William Henry Whitmore

An Essay on the Origin of the Names of Towns in

Massachusetts, Settled Prior to A.D. 1775

To which is prefixed an essay on the name of the town of Lexington

William Henry Whitmore

An Essay on the Origin of the Names of Towns in Massachusetts, Settled Prior to A.D. 1775
To which is prefixed an essay on the name of the town of Lexington

ISBN/EAN: 9783337219727

Printed in Europe, USA, Canada, Australia, Japan

Cover: Foto ©ninafisch / pixelio.de

More available books at **www.hansebooks.com**

AN ESSAY

ON THE ORIGIN OF THE

NAMES OF TOWNS IN MASSACHUSETTS,

SETTLED PRIOR TO A.D. 1775.

TO WHICH IS PREFIXED

AN ESSAY ON THE NAME OF THE TOWN OF LEXINGTON.

BY

WILLIAM HENRY WHITMORE.

Reprinted from the Proceedings of the Massachusetts Historical Society for 1872-3.

BOSTON:

PRESS OF JOHN WILSON AND SON.

1873.

ON THE ORIGIN OF THE

NAMES OF TOWNS IN MASSACHUSETTS,

SETTLED PRIOR TO A.D. 1775.

TO WHICH IS PREFIXED

AN ESSAY ON THE NAME OF THE TOWN OF LEXINGTON.

BY

WILLIAM HENRY WHITMORE.

Reprinted from the Proceedings of the Massachusetts Historical Society for 1872-3.

BOSTON:
PRESS OF JOHN WILSON AND SON.
1873.

PREFACE.

THE peculiar arrangement of the following essays is due to the fact that they were thus prepared for presentation to the Historical Society. I had devoted considerable time to the consideration of the whole subject; but the origin of the name of the town of Lexington had a special interest for me, and I devoted to its investigation an amount of space which could not be afforded to that of other towns.

I have but one suggestion to add to those in the Lexington pamphlet; and that is, to point out that farther investigation showed that Sunderland was named after Lexington. The considerations which I have urged on page 20 tend, I think, to strengthen my case against the probability of the naming of a town in honor of any English statesman before the time of Governor Shute.

As this is the first attempt of which I have knowledge to trace the origin of our Massachusetts town-names, I cannot expect that it is entirely correct, or that it will prevent others from pursuing the subject. I trust, on the contrary, that it will incite others to investigate this very interesting branch of local history, and shall be amply repaid if thereby the continuance of common error is prevented.

W. H. W.

BOSTON, June, 1873.

ON THE ORIGIN

OF THE

NAME OF THE TOWN OF LEXINGTON.

In the admirable History of the Town of Lexington, by our learned associate, Hon. Charles Hudson, there will be found on pp. 422–424 his explanation of the origin of the name. The subject is worth a little attention, since, as the author says, "Lexington has become a watchword for freemen throughout British America"; and "twenty-two counties, cities, and towns of the name are scattered over every section of our wide country."

There being confessedly no authoritative explanation of the reason for the selection of this name, when the town was incorporated, March 20, 1712–13, Mr. Hudson considers that it was given in honor of Robert Sutton, second and last Lord Lexington, who died in 1723. This surmise is fortified by the assertion that "a custom is said to have prevailed in Massachusetts in those days, when a town was incorporated, to pass the Order or Act, and send it to the Governor with a blank for the name to be filled by him." He adds that the then governor was Joseph Dudley, who was a friend and relative of Lord Lexington, the Dudleys being of the Sutton family; and so the name "given to this town would, if given by the Legislature, be a compliment to the Governor, and if given by the Governor himself would be a compliment to his friend and relative."

To most of these assertions I must oppose a denial. In the first place there is no proof that Governor Joseph Dudley was related to Lord Lexington. All that is known of the pedigree of the American Dudleys is, that Governor Thomas Dudley was born in the town of Northampton, and was the son of a Captain Roger Dudley who was slain in the wars. Here the pedigree stops absolutely, and thus far no additional light has been thrown on it. It has been supposed, but never proved, that Roger Dudley was the great-grandson of Edward, second Baron Dudley ; but even if this were true, the connection with Sutton is very remote. It is generally held by the heralds that Rowland de Sutton of Aram married about A.D. 1250 the sister and co-heir of Robert, Baron Lexinton, a title which was soon extinct. In one line from this marriage came the Suttons, — Barons Sutton of Dudley, created in 1342 ; and in another the Suttons of Aram, created Baron Lexington of Aram in 1645.

If Governor Dudley's pedigree were substantiated, he would have to reckon five generations to Edward, second Baron Dudley ; two more to John Dudley, fourth Baron Sutton of Dudley, and first Baron Dudley ; and at least eight generations more, or fifteen in all, to find an ancestor in common with Lord Lexington.

Considering the glories which rightly cling to the name of Dudley in England, we may well doubt if Governor Dudley would have sought so remote a kinsman to honor with a compliment.

As to their being acquaintances and friends, there is no reason to suppose it. I believe that no document or report points to any such personal knowledge, and it must be dismissed as a pardonable but unproved surmise.

In the next place, there is no evidence that Governor Dudley had any thing to do with naming the town. I have made very careful search in regard to this matter of names given by our Provincial Governors, and I am convinced that it became a practice only under Governor Bernard. Many of the towns were incorporated by resolves, and not by special acts ; and I have examined all of the engrossed acts of town incorporations under the second charter. I will not take the space to detail the results of my search, but will repeat that the custom of passing the act with the name in blank did not begin before 1732. In that year (Mass. Rec. xv. pp. 265, 271, 280) the acts for Townsend and Harvard were passed in blank, sent down engrossed, read three times and passed to be enacted still in blank. The name of Harvard is written in by Secretary Willard. After this time it became of more frequent occurrence, and the earliest handwriting of a governor on the engrossed act is possibly that of Belcher. My present impression is that Shirley wrote three or four. When we come to Bernard, however, the case is different. During his term, 1760–1769, there were 39 towns formed in Massachusetts, 32 by act, and of these 26 have the names written in by Bernard. In what is now Maine, 10 towns were made, 6 by act, of which

Bernard wrote 5. Governor Hutchinson acted in the same way. Under his rule in both States 26 new towns were created, 16 by act, and of these 13 were written by him.

It seems, then, that Mr. Hudson was rightly informed that the Provincial Governors did supply largely the local nomenclature. But he was in error in supposing that this was the case in 1713, as the custom was not in force till a half century later.

To sum up thus far, it seems that Mr. Hudson's reasoning is wrong, because in the first place there is no proof that Dudley was acquainted with Lord Lexington; secondly, no evidence that they were relatives at all; thirdly, if related, the connection was extremely remote; and fourthly, a certainty that the Governor, as such, had nothing to do with the name, and no evidence that Dudley, as an individual, had any connection with it.

But, after all, the name had some reason for being. The large English Gazetteers do not contain the name of Lexington as now existing, but refer it to the present name of Laxton. This is a parish in Nottinghamshire, and is otherwise called Laxington with Moorhouse. It is ten miles from Newark, contains 3,610 acres, 126 houses, and in 1841 the population was 642.

This is clearly the source of our name, since the Lord Lexington derives his title from this place; and so Mr. Hudson's theory would give us the same derivation at second-hand.

In Thoroton's History of Nottinghamshire, published in 1677, p. 373, he treats of "Laxton, Lexington, and Moorhouse." It appears that there were two manors, one termed Laxton and the other Lexington; but possibly these are mere variations of the same word, otherwise termed Lessinton and Lexinton. In Henry III.'s time, Robert de Lexington, Baron of Tuxford, was a judge; his brother, John de Lexinton, was Lord Chancellor, 1238 and 1247; and Henry de Lessinton, another brother, was Bishop of Lincoln in 1254. This family, however, ended in the male line in that generation; and one of the sisters of Lord Lexinton married Robert de Sutton of Aram, and inherited a part at least of the property.

After twelve generations the representation of the family came to Robert Sutton of Aram, who was in 1645 raised to the peerage. In memory of the great family of which he was a co-heir, he took the title of Lord Lexington of Aram. His son, the second Lord, died in 1723, leaving an only daughter, Bridget, wife of the third Duke of Rutland. The title became extinct, but the estates came eventually to George Manners, third son of Bridget, who took the additional name of Sutton. From him were descended Charles Manners-Sutton, Archbishop of Canterbury; Thomas Manners-Sutton, Lord Chancellor of Ireland, created Lord Manners in 1807; and Charles Manners-Sutton, Speaker of the House 1817–1834, created Viscount Canterbury in 1835.

The question still remains, Why was this name chosen in 1713 for a little town in Massachusetts? Having removed the special and specious reasons adduced by Mr. Hudson, was the then Lord Lexington a man worthy of such a compliment, and was it customary then to name our towns for distinguished Englishmen?

As to the first point, I cannot find that this nobleman was pre-eminent. In 1851 there was published a volume entitled "The Lexington Papers," being extracts from his correspondence, then recently discovered by accident.

It seems that Lord Lexington was made a member of the Privy Council in 1691; was employed in the Diplomatic Service; was Envoy to Vienna, 1694–1697; one of the Council of Trade and Plantations, 1699–1705, but not after that time; one of the Lords of the Bedchamber; Ambassador to Spain, 1712–1714; and was "named as likely to hold high office in the Government about to be formed under the auspices of Lord Bolingbroke," when Queen Anne died. He was severely censured in the Report of Mr. Walpole's committee, but escaped the impeachment which befell Oxford, Bolingbroke, and Strafford. The remainder of his life was passed in retirement, and he died Sept. 19, 1723, aged sixty-two years.

Waiving the point whether Lord Lexington was so distinguished that his name would be selected, — and I for one should contend that he was not, — I desire to call attention to another important part of the case. It is clear that if he were distinguished at all in 1713, it was as a member of Bolingbroke's party, the ultra Jacobites, the Tories who were ready to place the Stuart Pretender on the throne instead of King George.

But Hutchinson, under date of 1714 (Hist. of Mass., ed. 1767, vol. ii. p. 209), writes as follows: —

"The secret designs of Queen Ann's last ministry were nowhere more suspected, nor more dreaded, than in the Massachusets; and the first of August was nowhere celebrated with greater joy during the whole of the king's reign."

I think, therefore, that we may safely assume that, if the Legislature of Massachusetts desired to compliment any English statesman, the choice would not have fallen on one of Bolingbroke's friends.

Having attempted to show that, if a custom prevailed of naming towns for living statesmen, the choice would not have fallen on Lord Lexington, I have farther to urge that there is no evidence of such a custom. Of course we may leave out of consideration the towns named under the first charter, many of the names evidently being given by the emigrants. But from 1689 to 1724 it is hardly possible to find any trace of a custom of honoring living Englishmen in this way. The towns named were Little Compton, Freetown, Rochester, Tiverton, Harwich, Attleborough, all before 1695 ; Framingham (1700), Dracut (1702), Brookline (1705), Plympton (1707), Truro (1709), Pembroke, Norton, Needham, Weston, Dighton, Abington, Chatham, Leicester, Northfield, Rutland, Lexington (1711–1713), Medway, Oxford, Chilmark, Sunderland, Sutton, Littleton, Hopkinton (1713–1715), Westborough, Brookfield, and Bellingham (1717–1719). From 1724 — when Holliston, Walpole, and Methuen were named — we begin to see a system in use of complimenting distinguished Englishmen ; but before this I can see no trace of the custom. In this list of thirty-two towns, Abingdon or Abington and Lexington are the only two which could reasonably be considered especially personal. Oxford was indeed the title of the Prime Minister ; but it occurs with Leicester and Rutland, and we may well consider that the English counties were meant. Sunderland is the name of a large seaport as well as of a peerage, and Sutton * is the name of sixty English parishes. As to Abington, there was, indeed, living in 1711 Montagu Bertie, second Earl of Abingdon, one of over sixty Privy Councillors. As there are three or four Abingtons in England, I prefer to seek the origin of our name in one of them, rather than to suppose this utterly obscure peer was thus selected for honor.

I hope, then, that having settled that Governor Dudley had nothing to do with giving the name, I have shown that the Legislature before 1724 did not have a custom of selecting

---

* At first sight the names Sutton, Lexington, Leicester, and Rutland seem to favor Mr. Hudson's theory. But I have explained Sutton and Leicester, and I would add that the marriage of the heiress of Lexington to the Duke of Rutland was not until 1717, or some four years after the naming of our towns. Coincidences bear many interpretations.

the names of English statesmen for the new towns, and that
certainly had they made such a choice, it would not in 1713
have fallen on a high Tory like Lord Lexington.   I trust that
I have wholly disproved the supposition to which my learned
friend was driven by the necessity of accounting in some way
for the name of our famous town.   I would add that the derivation was a very plausible one, and only to be questioned
after an examination of the whole subject of our local nomenclature, which could hardly be demanded of the historian of
a town.

But if we reject the mediation of Lord Lexington, can any
reason be given for the choice of this obscure hamlet in Nottinghamshire for commemoration here?   I will propound a
theory in reply, confessing, however, that it is not supported
by the desired evidences.   It is very certain that our first settlers gave to their new homes, in many instances, the names
of the villages whence they had emigrated.   We do not find
the cities and great provincial centres thus remembered, but
the little places in which their recollections centred.   Research
in such cases proves that some one of the settlers had thus
the honor and pleasure of perpetuating the name of the home
of his youth.   I venture to suggest that in the same way Lexington may have been the renewal of the name of the English
home of some one of the settlers.   Although not incorporated
till 1713, Lexington was set off as a precinct in 1691, in
accordance with a petition made in 1682.   At that time the
settlement was known as the North Precinct or Cambridge
Farms; terms of no particular force, being merely descriptive
of a part of Cambridge.

A search of the parish records of Lexington or Laxton,
England, made by Colonel Joseph L. Chester, shows clearly
that, with one exception, none of the first settlers at our Lexington bore names found there.   In the order for the boundary
line in 1684, confirmed in 1691, it was placed " on the south
side of Francis Whitmore's house towards the town of Cambridge aforesaid "; that is, so as to enclose his house in the
new town.   In 1713 the order incorporating the town of Lexington recited this order, and therefore repeats the name of
Francis Whitmore.

Without putting too much stress on this prominence given
to his name, it is fair to point out that the limits of the town
were fixed during the lifetime of Francis Whitmore, and that
the incorporated name was taken during the residence of his
son Samuel on the same land.

Francis Whitmore was one of the early colonists, born in 1625, presumably in England, and could it be shown that he was born in Lexington, England, it would be a moral certainty that we have found the cause of the name here.

Unfortunately the evidence on this point is still wanting; but something can be said in favor of the probability. Early in the seventeenth century the chief family at Laxton, Notts, was that of Roos. Francis Roos, of Laxton, who died in 1577, had, besides male descendants who continued the name, a daughter, who married Thomas Whitmore. Their son was Rev. Francis Whitmore, of Bingham, county Notts, whose son, Francis Whitmore, was of London chiefly, but whose will, proved in 1649, styles him of Laxton.

We can say, then, that there was in 1649 a Francis Whitmore, of Laxton or Lexington, England, and a Francis Whitmore, of Cambridge, Mass., at the same time. That this last-named Francis lived in that part of Cambridge, which, in the lifetime of his son, was called Lexington. However fallacious coincidences may be, the absence of all other reasons for the naming of this town may lead us to attach some importance to this concurrence of names. When we find a town named, as Groton was, by one of the emigrants in honor of his own home, the connection is evident. On the other hand, when we find Colonel Richard Lee, an emigrant to Virginia, naming his plantations Ditchley and Stratford, we feel sure that he must be a relative of the Lees of those places in England. In the case of Lexington, we have neither the certainty that Francis Whitmore named it, which would argue that he belonged to the family there at Laxton, nor any proof that he was of that origin, which would make it reasonable to think he revived the name of Lexington here. All that can be said is, that there was some reason for the name; if Francis Whitmore were born at Laxton, England, that would be sufficient reason; that Lord Lexington had nothing to do with the matter; and so for lack of certainty the question must still remain unsettled.

ON THE ORIGIN

OF THE

NAMES OF TOWNS IN MASSACHUSETTS.

ON THE ORIGIN OF THE NAMES OF TOWNS IN MASSACHUSETTS.

In a previous essay I have mentioned that the origin of the names of our towns is quite obscure; but, believing that much may be discovered still as to the causes which led to their selection, I have prepared the following lists.

In the first list will be found the earliest date at which the name of any town occurs. Usually, this will be the date of its incorporation; but not invariably, as some settlements were first known by Indian names, — as precincts or parts of other towns, — or even by a name afterwards changed and lost.

Our history is naturally divided into three parts: first, the Colonial period, from the settlement to the administration of Andros; second, the Provincial period, under the Second Charter; third, the time since the Revolution, or the period of the State. Each of these periods has a political and social character of its own, and, as will be shown, each has had a distinctive nomenclature for its new settlements.

In the first period we find, as might be expected, that the colonists gave to their towns names chiefly of English origin. Of the sixty towns named before 1690 in Massachusetts Colony, not one retained an Indian name; while Scituate and Monomoy are the only two examples in Plymouth Colony. Although both colonies were Puritanic, Salem and Rehoboth were the only Scriptural names.

Not only did our forefathers select English names, but they chose them without any plan of commemorating the more prominent cities and towns of England. The most marked peculiarity of these early names is, that their English namesakes are so obscure. We feel at once assured that these names were not adopted by chance, or on general grounds; but that each represents some local affection, some individual reason, which may still be traced out by careful study. In most instances, doubtless, some settler at the new town was an emigrant from the English village; and, since our knowledge of the origin of the early colonists is so scanty, we may find that the study of our local nomenclature will be a valuable source of information to the genealogist.

List of Towns in Massachusetts Colony.

[The references are to the printed volumes of Records.]

1.	Salem	Aug. 23, 1630, first mentioned.	I. 73
2.	Charlestown	do. do.	do.
3.	Boston	Sept. 7, 1630, named.	I. 75
4.	Dorchester	do. do.	do.
5.	Watertown	do. do.	do.
6.	Roxbury	Sept. 28, 1630, first mentioned.	I. 77
7.	Medford	do. do.	do.
8.	Marblehead	July 2, 1633, do.	I. 106
9.	Ipswich	Aug. 5, 1634, named.	I. 123
10.	Newbury	May 6, 1635, do.	I. 146

11.	Hingham	Sept. 2, 1635, named.		I. 156
12.	Weymouth . . .	do. do.		do.
13.	Concord	Sept. 3, 1635, do.		I. 15',
14.	Dedham	Sept. 8, 1636, do.		I. 18)
15.	Cambridge . . .	do. do.		do.
16.	Lynn	Nov. 20, 1637, do.		I. 21;
17.	Sudbury	Sept. 4, 1639, do.		I. 27''
18.	Hampton	do. do.		do.
19.	Rowley	do. do.		do.
	Colchester . . .	do. do.	(see No. 21.)	do.
20.	Braintree	May 13, 1640, do.		I. 291
21.	Salisbury	Oct. 7, 1640, do.		I. 305
22.	Haverhill	June 2, 1641, first mentioned.		I. 319
23.	Springfield . . .	do. do.		I. 320
24.	Gloucester . . .	June 14, 1642, do.		II. 14
25.	Woburn	Sept. 27, 1642, named.		II. 28
26.	Wenham . . .	Sept. 7, 1643, do.		II. 44
27.	Reading	May 29, 1644, do.		II. 73
28.	Hull	do. do.		II. 74
29.	Manchester . . .	May 14, 1645, do		II. 109
30.	Andover	May 6, 1646, do.		III. 73
31.	Malden	May 11, 1649, do.		III. 162
32.	Medfield	May 23, 1650, do.		III. 188
33.	Topsfield	Oct. 18, 1650, do.		IV. pt. I. 33
34.	Lancaster. . . .	May 18, 1653, do.		III. 303
35.	Groton	May 29, 1653, do.	•	IV. pt. I. 235
36.	Chelmsford . . .	do. do.		IV. pt. I. 237
37.	Billerica	do. do.		do.
38.	Northampton . .	May 16, 1656, first mentioned.		III. 400
39.	Marlborough . .	May 31, 1660, named.		IV. pt. 1, 424
40.	Hadley	May 22, 1661, do.		IV. pt. 2, 11
41.	Milton	May 7, 1662, do.		IV. pt. 2, 51
42.	Mendon	May 15, 1667, do.		IV. pt. 2, 341
43.	Amesbury . . .	May 27, 1668, do.		IV. pt. 2, 376
44.	Beverly	Nov. 7, 1668, do.		IV. pt. 2, 407
45.	Westfield . . .	May 19, 1669, do.		IV. pt. 2, 432
46.	Hatfield	May 31, 1670, do.		IV. pt. 2, 460
47.	Brookfield . . .	Oct. 15, 1673, do.		do. 568
48.	Wrentham . . .	do. do.		do. 569
49.	Dunstable . . .	do. do.		do. 570
50.	Southfield (Suffield),	June 3, 1674, do.		V. 13
51.	Sherburne . . .	Oct. 7, 1674, do.		V. 23
52.	Bradford	Oct. 13, 1675, first mentioned.		V. 56
53.	Deerfield	Oct. 22, 1677, do.		V. 167

Plymouth Colony.

1*.	Plymouth	Dec. 11, 1620, settled.		
2*.	Scituate	July 1, 1633, first mentioned.		I. 13
3*.	Duxbury	Jan. 5, 1635-6, do.		I. 36
4*.	Sandwich	March 6, 1637-8, do.		I. 80
5*.	Yarmouth	Jan. 7, 1638-9, do.		I. 108
6*.	Barnstable	June 4, 1639, do.		I. 126
7*.	Taunton	March 3, 1639-40, do.		I. 141
8*.	Marshfield	June 7, 1642, do.		II. 40
9*.	Rehoboth	Oct. 28, 1645, do.		II. 91
10*.	Eastham	June 5, 1651, do.		II. 168
11*.	Bridgewater	June 3, 1656, do.		III. 101
12*.	Dartmouth	June 8, 1664, do.		IV. 65
13*.	Swansey	March 5, 1667-8, do.		IV. 175
14*.	Middleborough	June 1, 1669, do.		V. 19
15*.	Manamoyet (now Chatham)	March 8, 1678-9, named.		VI. 4
16*.	Bristol	Oct. 28, 1681, do.		VI. 87

54.	Stow	May 16, 1683, named.	V. 409
55.	Enfield	do. do.	V. 410
56.	Worcester . . .	Oct. 15, 1684, do.	V. 460
57.	Boxford	1685?	
58.	Woodstock . . .	March 13, 1689-90,	* Order, Mass. Rec. VI. 126
59.	Newtown	Dec. 8, 1691,	* do. do. VI. 207
60.	Oxford		
17*.	Little Compton	June 6, 1682, named.	VI. 89
18*.	Freetown	July, 1683, do.	VI. 113
19*.	Rochester	June 4, 1686, do.	VI. 189
20*.	Falmouth	do. 1686.	VI. 189

Towns in 1695.

On the first tax list under the new Charter, Sept. 14, 1695, we find the names of 83 towns ; viz., 13 in Suffolk, 17 in Essex, 17 in Middlesex, 7 in Hampshire, 6 in Plymouth, 7 in Barnstable, 8 in Bristol, 4 in the Islands, and 4 in York.

There were also Dunstable, Deerfield, and Woodstock named at this period as "frontier towns." Brookfield and Worcester had been abandoned. Tiverton, incorporated under the new *régime*, was included ; but Hampton was omitted, having been ceded to New Hampshire. This would make 88 towns existing before Tiverton, which would be No. 89 in the full account.

The lists are as follows : —

SUFFOLK.	ESSEX.	MIDDLESEX.	HAMPSHIRE.
3. Boston.	1. Salem.	2. Charlestown.	23. Springfield.
6. Roxbury.	9. Ipswich.	5. Watertown.	38. Northampton.
4. Dorchester.	10. Newbury.	15. Cambridge.	40. Hadley.
41. Milton.	19. Rowley.	13. Concord.	46. Hatfield.
20. Brantrey.	21. Salisbury.	25. Woburn.	50. Southfield.
12. Weymouth.	43. Amesbury.	39. Marlboro.	45. Westfield.
11. Hingham.	22. Haverhill.	35. Groton.	55. Enfield.
28. Hull.	30. Andover.	27. Reading.	
14. Dedham.	52. Bradford.	86. Chelmsford.	
32. Medfield.	57. Boxford.	17. Sudbury.	
48. Wrentham.	33. Topsfield.	31. Malden.	
42. Mendon.	8. Marblehead.	7. Medford.	
60. Oxford.	16. Lynn.	35. Billerica.	
	26. Wenham.	34. Lancaster.	
	44. Beverly	54. Stow.	
	24. Gloucester.	59. Newtown.	
	29. Manchester.	51. Sherburne.	

PLYMOUTH.	BARNSTABLE.	BRISTOL.	M. VINEYARD.
1*. Plymouth.	6*. Barnstable.	16*. Bristol.	Edgartown.
2*. Situate.	5*. Yarmouth.	7*. Taunton.	Tisbury.
3*. Duxbury.	10*. Eastham.	12*. Dartmouth.	Chilmark.
8*. Marshfield.	4*. Sandwich.	18*. Freetown.	Nantucket.
11*. Bridgewater.	20*. Falmouth.	9*. Rehoboth.	
14*. Middleboro'.	15*. Monomoy.	13*. Swanzey.	
	19*. Rochester.	17*. Little Compton.	
		89. Tiverton.	

YORK.
York.
Wells.
Kittery.
Isle of Shoals.

* These references are to the manuscript volumes in the Secretary of State's Office, Boston.

I will next proceed to state such facts as I have found relative to the reasons for naming these Colonial towns, taking the places in chronological order.

Presumed Reason for the Names of Towns in Massachusetts Colony.

1. *Salem.*   A Scriptural name.
2. *Charlestown.*   Named from Charles River, a name given by Captain Smith. (Frothingham's Hist. p. 21.)
3. *Boston.*   According to Dudley (Drake's Hist. p. 89), the first settlers named the place Boston, "which we intended to have done the place we first resolved on." Many of the emigrants were from Lincolnshire.
4. *Dorchester.*   Blake, writing a century after the settlement, says, "Why they called it Dorchester, I never heard; but there was some of Dorcet Shire, and some of y° Town of Dorchester, that settled here; and it is very likely it might be in Honour of y° aforesaid Rev⁴. Mr. White, of Dorchester."
5. *Watertown.*   Savage (Winthrop's Hist. i. 43) conjectures that the name was given by Saltonstall, and was copied from Waterton, county York. But it may well have been derived from the natural features of the place.
6. *Roxbury.*   Spelled also Rocksbury.   Probably named from its appearance.
7. *Medford.*   Called Meadford by Dudley. It is termed Metford in the deeds of Cradock's widow; and there was a hamlet of that name (now Hayford) very near to Caverswell, the seat of the Cradock family.
8. *Marblehead.*   "Salem was first called Marble harbor from the quantity of that stone there, and the name rested with Marblehead." (Felt's Salem, i. 6.)
9. *Ipswich.*   So named "in acknowledgment of the great honor and kindness done to our people which took shipping there," says Winthrop. (Hist. i. 164.) Ipswich, Eng., is in co. Suff.
10. *Newbury.*   Named from Newbury, co. Berks, Eng., where Rev. Thomas Parker, the first minister of this town, had preached. (Coffin's Hist. p. 1.)
11. *Hingham.*   Named from Hingham, co. Norfolk, whence most of its early settlers came. (N. E. Hist. and Gen. Register, xv. 25–27.)
12. *Weymouth.*   Unknown; but possibly in honor of Captain George Waymouth, the navigator. It is to be noted that, 20th March, 1635, about one hundred persons are recorded at Weymouth, co. Dorset, Eng., as bound hither. (Register, xxv. 13.)
13. *Concord.*   A typical name.
14. *Dedham.*   It was first called Contentment by its inhabitants. In England, Dedham is a parish in co. Essex, 3 miles from Hadleigh.
15. *Cambridge.*   So named after the General Court decided to establish a college there.
16. *Lynn.*   Named in compliment to Rev. Samuel Whiting, first minister there, who had been a curate at Lynn Regis, co. Norfolk. (Newhall, Hist. p. 169.)
17. *Sudbury.*   There is, in England, a Sudbury in Derby; and also another in co. Suffolk, 11 miles from Hadleigh.
18. *Hampton.*   I think this is a revival of Capt. John Smith's name of Southampton for this locality. See his map of 1616.
19. *Rowley.*   Named by the first minister, Rev. Ezekiel Rogers, "who called the town Rowly; and continued in it about the same number of years that he had spent in that Rowly from whence he came, on the other side of the Atlantick ocean." (Magnalia.) It is in the East Riding of York, 7 miles from Beverley.
20. *Braintree.*   The English town of the name is in co. Essex, and is of great antiquity, and considerable local importance. It is 11 miles from Chelmsford.
21. *Salisbury.*   First called Colchester. At the session at which Salisbury was named, one of the deputies was Christopher Batte, who came from the

city of Salisbury, co. Wilts, says Savage. Batte's cousin, Henry Byley of S., was also from the English city, and probably others. (See Register, xxiv. 78.)

22. *Haverhill.* Named for Haverhill, co. Essex, the birthplace of its first minister, Rev. John Ward. (Chuse, Hist. p. 40.)

23. *Springfield.* Named in honor of William Pynchon, one of the first settlers, "who had his mansion house at a town of that name near Chelmsford, in Essex, before he removed to New England." (Hubbard's Hist. in Mass. Hist. Soc. Coll., 2d Ser. vi. 308.)

24. *Gloucester.* Perhaps named in honor of its first minister, Rev. Richard Blinman. (Caulkin's New London, pp. 114–117.)

25. *Woburn.* Probably named for Woburn, co. Bedford, Eng., a town chiefly famous for containing Woburn Abbey, the noted seat of the Russells, Dukes of Bedford. A John Russell was one of the earliest settlers in our town, and there was also here Richard Russell, a prominent citizen of Charlestown. Either may have suggested the name.

26. *Wenham.* The first minister of this town was Rev. John Fisk, who was born, says Cotton Mather, in the parish of St. James, in the northerly corner of the county of Suffolk. Wenham, co. Suffolk, is at the extreme southern part, near Ipswich. Still, as the Fisks, of whom four brothers came hither, besides others of the name, were eminently a Suffolk family, and largely concerned in the affairs of our town, the evidence seems strong that they gave the name.

27. *Reading.* Unknown. Reading in Berkshire, Eng., was a place of considerable importance, the birthplace of Archbishop Laud. It was the scene of considerable fighting in 1642–1644.

28. *Hull.* Kingston-upon-Hull, commonly called Hull, in the East Riding of York, is a county of itself, and a well-known seaport. It was strongly in favor of the Parliament when the civil war broke out. It stood two severe assaults from the royal troops, but was never taken.

29. *Manchester.* The famous city of this name in Lancashire has but recently risen to its present importance. In 1644–5, however, the Duke of Manchester was the chief commander of the Parliament troops ; and I am inclined to consider that Reading, Hull, and Manchester were names suggested by the events then occurring in England.

30. *Andover.* The English town in co. Hants, 18 miles from Salisbury and Amesbury.

31. *Malden.* In England we find Malden, a little parish in co. Surrey ; and Maldon, a borough, port, and market-town in co. Essex. There is also Maulden, a parish in co. Bedford.

32. *Medfield.* This name, I believe, does not appear in the English gazetteers. The town was set off from Dedham. It is termed in the record of incorporation .Meadfield; and the name may thus be a descriptive one, as Barber reports the tradition.

33. *Topsfield.* In England, Topesfield is a parish in the county of Essex. Governor Symonds owned land there, and undoubtedly gave this name. (See Appleton's "Ancestry of Priscilla Baker," p. 77.)

34. *Lancaster.* The capital of the county of Lancashire, and one of the most familiar names in England.

35. *Groton.* The petition for this grant was headed by Deane Winthrop, and the name was of course given by him in memory of the family possessions in the county of Suffolk, Eng.

36. *Chelmsford.* The English town is in the county of Essex, 29 miles from London, 8 from Billericay.

37. *Billerica.* Billericay, co. Essex, is a market-town 23 miles from London, of no special note. We know that at least one family, the Ruscoes, came from this place.

38. *Northampton.* The name of an English county, and of its chief town.

39. *Marlborough.* At this time Marlborough, co. Wilts, was a place of no great importance. The title since taken by the Churchills has made it famous. We know of several emigrants from this place.

40. *Hadley.* We find a Hadleigh in co. Suffolk ; and one in Essex, 10 miles

from Billericay. There are also Hadley-with-Blagrave, co. Berks, and Hadley-Monken, co. Middlesex.

41. *Milton.* It would be pleasant to think that this town was named in honor of John Milton, but I know of no reasons in favor of the surmise. The name, Milton, alone or with others, belongs to over twenty parishes and towns in England.

42. *Mendon.* By the records it appears that this name was meant for Mendam or Mendham. The English town is in co. Suffolk.

43. *Amesbury.* The English town is 7 miles from Salisbury, co. Wilts.

44. *Beverly.* This is the name of a large town in the East Riding of York. In 1671, according to Stone's History, pp. 16–18, Roger Conant and thirty-four others petitioned to have the name changed, "because, we being but a small place, it hath caused on us a constant nickname of *Beggarly.*" He adds, "I being the first that had house in Salem (and neither had any hand in naming either that or any other town), and myself, with those that were then with me, being all from the western part of England, desire this western name of Budleigh, a market-town in Devonshire, and near unto the sea, as we are here in this place, and where myself was born." He also says that "no order was given, or consent by the people to their agent, for any name, until we were sure of being a town granted, in the first place." The request was refused.

45. *Westfield.* Barber says that it was first proposed to call this town Streamfield, because situated between two streams; but it was afterwards named from its site as the most westerly plantation. ·

46. *Hatfield.* There are parishes of this name in the counties of Hereford, Hertford, York, and *Essex.* Yet it may well be asked if this name was not in some way connected with Hadley, from which it was set off.

47. *Brookfield.* A name clearly derived from the local features.

48. *Wrentham.* There is a small parish of this name in co. Suffolk, from which came Thomas Paine and John Thurston. Thomas Thurston, a grandson, was of Wrentham, Mass.

49. *Dunstable.* In England we have Dunstable, co. Bedford, a considerable market-town. The history of the town states (p. 16), that the name was in honor of Mary, wife of Edward Tyng, whose son was one of the petitioners for the grant. This I doubt, since no one seems to know her maiden name or birthplace. But I do find that Robert Long, of Charlestown, came from Dunstable, co. Bedford, in 1635, with a large family. Among his children was Zachariah Long, whose name is also on the petition. This makes a very direct connection. It must be added, that Rev. William Symmes of Charlestown had been rector of Dunstable before his removal, and others of his flock may have followed him here.

50. *Suffield.* A local name here. The committee, on granting it, reported "that the name of the place may be Suffield (an abbreviation of Southfield), it being the southermost toune that either at present is or like to be in that country." It is now a part of Connecticut.

51. *Sherburne.* We find Sherborne, co. Dorset; also parishes of the name in Gloucester, Warwick, and Hants. Sherburn is the name of parishes in Durham and York.

52. *Bradford.* A large town in the West Riding of York bears this name.

53. *Deerfield.* Not an English name, and evidently of local origin here.

54. *Stow.* This name occurs repeatedly in England, in the counties of Lincoln, Salop, Huntington, *Suffolk,* Cambridge, Norfolk, Essex, Gloucester, Oxford, Bucks, Stafford, and Northampton.

55. *Enfield.* Enfield, co. Middlesex, is a parish 10 miles from London. This town now belongs to Connecticut.[a]

56. *Worcester.* A county in England. The battle of Worcester was Cromwell's "crowning mercy," and tradition states that the name was chosen here as a defiance to the king.

---

[a] There is now an Enfield in Hampshire county, formed in 1816. Holland (Hist. W. Mass. ii. 201) says the name was in honor of Robert Field. This is doubtless an error; and it was a revival of the old name, still existing also in Connecticut.

57. *Boxford.* In co. Suffolk, Boxford adjoins Groton.
58. *Woodstock.* Sewall writes, March 18, 1689–90, in his Diary : "I gave New-Roxbury the name of Woodstock, because of its nearness to Oxford, for the sake of Queen Elizabeth, and the notable meetings that have been held at the place bearing that name in England ; some of which Dr. Gilbert inform'd me of, when in England. It stands on a hill ; I saw it as (I) went to Coventry, but left it on the left hand. Some told Capt. Ruggles that I gave the name, and put words in his mouth to desire of me a Bell for the Town." It was transferred about 1750, to Connecticut.
59. *Newton.* Called New Town in the records until 1766, says Jackson. This was the early name of Cambridge, of which place Newton was a part.
60. *Oxford.* The exact date of this name is unknown. It was given between 16th May, 1683, when the grant of land was made, and 1695, when it occurs on the tax list.

In Plymouth County.

1*. *Plymouth.* Morton's Memorial says (p. 42) that it was so called on Smith's map, and was also so called because "Plimouth in O. E. was the last town they left in their native country, and for that they received many kindnesses from some Christians there."
2*. *Scituate.* An Indian name.
3*. *Duxbury.* Named in compliment to the Standishes of Duxbury Hall ; to which family Miles Standish probably claimed relationship.
4*. *Sandwich.* A seaport in Kent.
5*. *Yarmouth.* A seaport in Norfolk.
6*. *Burnstable.* A seaport in Devonshire, on the south side of the Bristol Channel.
7*. *Taunton.* Named by the chief founder, Miss Elizabeth Poole, whose family had long lived at Taunton, co. Somerset.
8*. *Marshfield.* Probably named from its site. It was first called Rexham, or Rexhame, which may refer to Wrexham, a town in co. Denbigh, North Wales.
9*. *Rehoboth.* A Scriptural name, given it by its pastor, Rev. Henry Newman, says Mather. (Magnalia, 3d book, chap. xv.)
10*. *Eastham.* There is a parish of this name in Cheshire, and another in Worcestershire.
11*. *Bridgewater.* In England, Bridgewater is in co. Somerset, 11 miles from Taunton.
12*. *Dartmouth.* A seaport in Devonshire, on the English Channel.
13*. *Swansey.* A seaport town in Glamorganshire, South Wales, about opposite Barnstable.
14*. *Middleborough.* There is a Middleborough in the North Riding of York ; yet our town may well be named from local causes.
15*. *Monomoy.* An Indian name.
16*. *Bristol.* The well-known city of the name is in co. Gloucester.
17*. *Little Compton.* Several places in England bear the name of Compton. The parish of Little Compton, co. Gloucester, is 3 miles from Stow.
18*. *Freetown.* Origin unknown.
19*. *Rochester.* An ancient city and seaport in Kent.
20*. *Falmouth.* A famous seaport in Cornwall.

Other Colonies.

North of the present limits of Massachusetts, there were four settlements remaining at the date of the Second Charter ; viz., York, Wells, Kittery, and Isle of Shoals. Of these, the earliest name is Kittery, given in 1647 : it is presumably an Indian name. York and Wells were named after the incorporation with Massachusetts, in 1652. As the county was called Yorkshire, the town was naturally called York. As to Wells, it is surmised that this was so named from the city in Somersetshire, because Thomas Gorges belonged to that county, and owned land in this town. The Isle of Shoals needs no explanation.

Islands.

Of lands annexed to Massachusetts, but which had already been named, Nantucket bore of course an Indian name. On Martin's Vineyard there were three towns, — Tisbury, Chilmark, and Edgartown. Of these names, given about 1671, Tisbury and Chilmark reproduce the two places in co. Wilts, a few miles west from Salisbury. Edgartown is of more difficult origin ; and I have never seen a solution attempted.

Classification of the Foregoing Names.

We can now proceed to some general conclusions in regard to these names. Salem, Charlestown, Boston, Ipswich, Concord, Cambridge, and possibly Hampton, were named on general grounds, irrespective of the local preferences of the emigrants. Watertown and Medford, most probably, were named to please Saltonstall and Cradock ; Newbury, Lynn, Rowley, and Haverhill, in honor of their first ministers ; Dorchester, Hingham, and probably Weymouth, were so named because many of their inhabitants came from those places. Roxbury and Marblehead were clearly named from their natural features.

Out of the first twenty-six names, we are left with Salisbury, Springfield, and Wenham, whose sponsors may be indicated with considerable accuracy ; and the following, whose origin is unknown: Dedham and Braintree (co. Essex, Eng.), Sudbury (co. Suff., Eng.), Gloucester (co. Glouc.), Woburn (co. Beds.).

We may imagine that Reading, Hull, and Manchester were souvenirs of the great Civil War, though this may be but a coincidence.

In the names from No. 30 to No. 43, Andover, Marlborough, and Amesbury go with Salisbury in Wiltshire names ; Malden, Topsfield, Chelmsford, Billericay, and Hadley, are in Essex: Lancaster and Northampton are English counties ; Medfield and Milton most probably are of local origin here ; Groton and Mendham are in Suffolk, Eng.

No. 44, Beverley, and No. 52, Bradford, are in Yorkshire ; Westfield, Brookfield, Suffield, Deerfield, and New-town originated here. Woodstock was named by Judge Sewall ; Dunstable evidently was named by emigrants from that place, or rather by their children. Wrentham, also, was settled by the descendants of emigrants from its English antetype ; Worcester and Oxford are English counties ; Stow (Market) and Boxford are Suffolk names ; Hatfield is in Essex, Enfield is in Middlesex, and Sherborn is indefinite.

The prevailing evidence is that, in the case of strictly local names, whether the sponsors be known or not, most of them were chosen from Essex and Suffolk. Each of these counties has nine representatives ; Wilts, three ; Dorset, three ; Middlesex, Berks, Beds, and Hants, one each. York has Beverley, Bradford, and Hull; Lancashire has one, if Manchester be counted. Of the English counties, five — Gloucester, Lancaster, Northampton, Worcester, and Oxford — gave names, apparently, to towns here.

Plymouth Colony.

Out of the twenty towns in this colony, Plymouth, Duxbury, Taunton, and probably Bridgewater, have been explained. Rehoboth is Scriptural; Scituate and Monomoy are Indian; Marshfield, Middleborough, and Freetown probably originated here; Little Compton and Eastham are difficult of explanation; Sandwich, Yarmouth, Barnstable, Dartmouth, Swansey, Bristol, Rochester, and Falmouth, are all English seaports. Of these eight, five are named on Captain Smith's map,* and we may fairly conclude that this circumstance led to the selection. Of course it is possible that emigrants came from each of these ports, but this does not seem so reasonable a conjecture.

SECOND CHARTER PERIOD.

We have already accounted for 60 towns in Massachusetts Colony, 20 in Plymouth, 4 in York, and 4 in the Islands: 88 towns in all. This agrees with the 83 towns taxed in 1695; and 6 towns untaxed, including No. 89, Tiverton, which was incorporated a few months before the tax was levied.†

For reasons which I trust are well founded, in proceeding with the lists of incorporations from 1694 to 1732, I treat these names as forming a distinct class. The principal reason is this: during this

---

* On the map by Captain John Smith, published in 1616, we find Plymouth, the Charles River, and Cape Ann named in the places they now occupy; and South Hampton may very fairly represent the site of Hampton. He also proposes Oxford and London, between Plymouth and Charles River; Falmouth, Bristol, and Barnstable, thence to Cape Ann; north of this, South Hampton, Hull, Boston, Ipswich, Dartmouth, Sandwich, and the Base. This brings him to Cape Elizabeth, which is at the mouth of the river Forth, and thereon are Leith, Cambridge, and Edinborough. East of this river he places St. John's Town and Norwich, and the great Pembroke's Bay, on which are Dumbarton and Aberdeen. South of Plymouth, at the bottom of the Bay, was Berwick; and Milford Haven was at the hook of Cape Cod, where Provincetown is.

† Massachusetts has lost, from time to time, various towns which had been incorporated by her authority. Thus, Hampton was ceded to New Hampshire, at the date of the Second Charter. In 1741, Litchfield, Nottingham, and Rumford, — all incorporated towns, — with parts of Methuen, Dracut, Dunstable, Salisbury, and Amesbury, were likewise transferred to New Hampshire. In 1747, Rhode Island obtained Little Compton, Tiverton, and Bristol, as well as the territory made by that colony into the towns of Warren and Cumberland. (See Arnold's History of Rhode Island, li. 157.)

A little later, about 1750, Connecticut appropriated the towns of Woodstock, Somers, Suffield, and Enfield, though she had before exchanged them with Massachusetts, and had received an equivalent.

Finally the formation of the State of Maine, in 1820, took from us 236 corporate towns, of which 34 were in existence before the Revolution.

The numbers which I have used in the following lists are therefore to be considered as of one value only. It is to be remembered that we have lost Nos. 18, 50, 55, 58, 89, 16*, and 17*, and that after 1750 these seven numbers are to be deducted. For a brief period 4 towns — viz., Somers, Litchfield, Nottingham and Rumford, not numbered in the lists — belonged to us. Hence the number denoting the relative position of any existing town must vary at different dates, and especially in regard to the purpose for which an enumeration is desired.

period, which covers the administrations of Phips, Bellomont, Dudley, Shute, and Burnet, the proposed name of the new town appears in the earliest stages of the legislation. We may therefore feel assured that we are treating of the names which the incorporators desired. Later, the process was changed, the acts or resolves passed both Houses in blank, and we only get the name when we find the bill returned approved by the Governor.

It is of course possible that the petitioners followed their bill, and had a name selected to meet their wishes. But it is indisputable that the later Governors, Bernard and Hutchinson, wrote in the names with their own hands, and it is very difficult to be sure of the handwriting in many of the earlier bills.*

I am inclined to make another division with the appointment of Governor Shute, who arrived here in 1716 and ruled until 1722. The first town clearly named in honor of a prime minister, I consider to be Sunderland, in 1718.† No one doubts of the certainty of the intention in the case of Walpole, in 1724. I think that there is more than a coincidence in the fact that, from the time when Englishmen began to come here as our governors, the names of contemporary English statesmen were given to our new towns. I can see no evidence that Governor Joseph Dudley had either the desire or the power to tender such compliments to any supposed English friends. Dudley was, moreover, a provincial ; and the custom of which we find evidence would be much more likely to have its origin in the aspirations or gratitude of an English office-holder.

Looking at the new towns incorporated between 1694 and 1724, we find the names agree with the previous classes. Brookline, Weston, Northfield, Littleton, and Westborough were of native origin. Pembroke, Rutland, and Leicester were county names at home. Hopkinton, Bellingham, Holliston, Dighton, and possibly Norton, were named for individuals ; as were Sunderland, Walpole, and Methuen. Harwich, Truro, and Chatham (with its allied name Medway) are seaports. Plympton and Chilmark are evidently connected with names already used here. Tiverton, Attleborough, Framingham, Abington, Dracut, Needham, Lexington, and Sutton belong to the class of little English villages remembered by emigrants thence.

* I have examined the engrossed acts in all the instances in which this form was adopted. In three instances, I think, Governor Shirley's handwriting appears in the naming of towns; but I am by no means confident of it. Earlier than this the secretary, or the engrossing clerk, supplies the name; and we can only surmise that it was by direction of the Council or the Governor. Bernard's handwriting is unmistakable. I feel reasonably sure that Hutchinson wrote the names I have assigned to him, though Oliver wrote a very similar hand, and may have filled in one or more names.

† Under Queen Anne (1702–1714), the heads of the administration were: 1702, Lord Godolphin; 1711, Earl of Oxford; 1714, Duke of Shrewsbury. Under George I.: 1714, Earl of Halifax; 1715, Sir Robert Walpole; 1717, Earl Stanhope; 1718, Earl of Sunderland; 1721–1742, Sir Robert Walpole.

Of our local administrations the terms were as follows: Sir William Phips, 1691–1694; Earl of Bellomont, 1699–1700; Joseph Dudley, 1702–1715; Samuel Shute, 1716–1722; William Burnet, 1728–1729; Jonathan Belcher, 1730–1741; William Shirley, 1741–1757; Thomas Pownall, 1757–1760; Francis Bernard, 1760–1769; Thomas Hutchinson, 1770–1774; Thomas Gage, 1774–1775.

Out of thirty names given between 1694 and 1724, but six seem to refer to the peerage,—Pembroke, Leicester, and Rutland, Abington, Lexington, and Sutton. It does not seem reasonable to refer the first three of these to the peerages rather than the counties. Sutton is a very common name, not then represented on the titles of the peerage, though a family name therein. Abington was a title borne by a very obscure peer, and Lexington has been elsewhere discussed.

We may say, then, that for about a century our ancestors gave names which may be divided into the following classes : one or two Scriptural and Indian names ; certain descriptive words originating here, as Marblehead, Westfield, Deerfield, Westborough, &c.; the names of English or Welsh counties; one or two names of Colonial celebrities. Lastly, a large number of places of little importance in England were remembered here, and the strong presumption is that these names were given by emigrants from those parishes.

From Sunderland to Townshend, 1732, the latter being the first of the towns incorporated in blank, we find little trouble. Provincetown, Stoughton, Dudley, and probably Easton, were of native origin ; Southborough, Middletown, Westford, and probably Brimfield, record local peculiarities ; Hanover and Lunenburg honored the king ; Walpole, Methuen, Kingston, Uxbridge, Shrewsbury, Bedford, Wilmington, Townshend, and Raynham (Lord Townshend's residence) all refer to prominent members of the English administration.

Towns named from 1694 to 1732.

[The references are to the printed volume of Provincial Laws.]

89.	Tiverton	June 14, 1694,	Act,	P. L. I.	174
90.	Harwich	Sept. 14, 1694,	Act,	do.	181
91.	Attleborough	Oct. 19, 1694,	Act,	do.	184
92.	Framingham	June 25, 1700,	Order,	Mass. Rec.a VII.	110
93.	Dracut	Feb. 26, 1701-2,	Resolve,	do. VII.	269
94.	Brookline	Nov. 13, 1705,	Order,	do. VIII.	167
95.	Plympton	June 4, 1707,	Order,	do. VIII.	299
96.	Truro	July 16, 1709,	Act,	P. L. I.	642
97.	Norton	June 12, 1711,	Act,	do. I.	676
98.	Needham	Nov. 5, 1711,	Order,	Mass. Rec. IX.	162
99.	Pembroke	March 21, 1711-12,	Act,	P. L. I.	685
100.	Dighton	May 30, 1712,	Order,	Mass. Rec. IX.	195
101.	Abington	June 10, 1712,	do.	do. IX.	205
102.	Chatham	June 11, 1712,	do.	do. IX.	207
103.	Weston	Jan. 1, 1712-3,	do.	do. IX.	250
104.	Lexington	March 20, 1712-13,	do.	do. IX.	259
105.	Medway	Oct. 24, 1713,	Act,	P. L. I.	722
106.	Leicester	Feb. 15, 1713-14,	Order,	Mass. Rec. IX.	351
107.	Northfield	Feb. 22, 1713-14,	do.	do. IX.	362
108.	Rutland	Feb. 23, 1713-14,	do.	do. IX.	366
109.	Chilmark	Oct. 30, 1714,	do.	do. IX.	429

Maine.

In this province were 1* Kittery, 2* York, 3* Wells, 4* Cape Porpoise (called Arundell in 1718), 5* Saco, 6* Scarboro', 7* Falmouth, and 8* North Yarmouth. The repeated abandonments of settlements, and changes of name, render the enumeration difficult; but I follow Williamson.

a These references are to the manuscript volumes in the Secretary's Office, Boston.

110. Sutton	June 21, 1715.			
111. Littleton. . . .	Dec. 3, 1715.			
112. Hopkinton . . .	Dec. 13, 1715.			
113. Westborough . .	Nov. 18, 1717.			
(Old) Brookfield . . .	Nov. 12, 1718.			
114. Sunderland . . .	do. do.	Order,	Mass. Rec.	X. 305
115. Bellingham . . .	Nov. 27, 1719.			
116. Holliston . . .	Dec. 3, 1724,	Act.		
117. Walpole	Dec. 10, 1724.			
118. Methuen . . .	Dec. 8, 1725,	Act.		
119. Stoneham . . .	Dec. 17, 1725,	Act.		
120. Easton	Dec. 21, 1725,	Act.		
121. Kingston . . .	June 16, 1726,	Act.		
122. Stoughton . . .	Dec. 22, 1726,	Act.		
123. Provincetown . .	June 14, 1727,	Act.		
124. Hanover	do. do.	Act.		
125. Uxbridge . . .	June 27, 1727,	Act.		
126. Southborough . .	July 6, 1727,	Act.		
127. Shrewsbury . .	Dec. 19, 1727,	Order.		
128. Middleton . . .	June 20, 1728.			
129. Lunenburg . . .	Aug. 1, 1728,	Act.		
130. Bedford	Sept. 23, 1729,	Act.		
131. Westford. . . .	do. do.	Act.		
132. Wilmington . . .	Sept. 25, 1730,	Act.		
133. Raynham . . .	April 2, 1731,	Act.		
134. Brimfield. . . .	July 14, 1731.			
135. Dudley	Feb. 2, 1731–32,	Act.		
136. Townshend . . .	June 29, 1732,	Act.		

9*. Berwick	9 June, 1713.	
10*. Georgetown	13 June, 1716.	

Names from 1732 to 1774.

In considering the names of towns subsequent to 1718, it will perhaps be well to take the periods covered by the administration of each of our Governors.

SAMUEL SHUTE, 1716–1722.

In this period we have Sunderland.

LT.-GOV. WILLIAM DUMMER, 1723–1728.

In this we find Walpole, Methuen; Kingston, Hanover, Uxbridge and Shrewsbury.

WILLIAM BURNET, 1728–1729.

Lunenburg and Bedford.

JONATHAN BELCHER, 1730–1741.

Wilmington, Raynham, Townshend, Sheffield, Halifax, Tewksbury, Berkeley, Grafton, Hardwicke, Bolton, and Blandford. Out of 24 names, 11 are directly derived from the titles of prominent Englishmen. Dudley, Harvard, Holden, were also named for persons. Upton, Acton, Waltham, Chelsea, Sturbridge, Stockbridge, Wareham, Leominster, Western, and Brimfield are untraced.

WILLIAM SHIRLEY, 1741–1757.

Pelham, Douglas, were probably English titles.   Shirley, Pepperrell, and Montague were souvenirs of our French War.   New Braintree, South Hampton, South Hadley, and New Salem need no explanation; and Greenfield is probably of local origin here.   Spencer, Granville, Lincoln, Petersham, seem to be derived from the peerage.   Greenwich and Charlton are in doubt.

THOMAS POWNALL, 1757–1760.

Danvers, Amherst, New Marlborough, Egremont, and Monson were named in this period.   Of these Danvers was given in honor of the Governor's patron, Amherst commemorates a general, and Egremont and Monson are referable to the peerage.

FRANCIS BERNARD, 1760–1769.

Governor Bernard was here from August, 1760, to August, 1769.   In that time were named 39 towns in this State, viz.: —

Pittsfield, Great Barrington, Coleraine, Belchertown, Shutesbury, Ware, Sandisfield, Tyringham, Bernardston, Athol, Templeton, Chesterfield, Oakham, Natick, Warwick, Marshpee, Wilbraham, Wellfleet, Newbury Port, Fitchburg, Winchendon, Paxton, Royalston, Ashburnham, Sharon, Becket, Lanesborough, Williamstown, Ashfield, Charlemont, Chester, Northborough, Lenox, Ashby, Hubbardstown, Conway, Granby, Shelburne, Worthington.

And also in Maine, 10, viz.: —

Windham, Buxton, Bowdoinham, Topsham, Gorham, Boothbay, Bristol, Cape Elizabeth, Lebanon, and Sandford.

Of the 39, 32 were incorporated by act, and of these all but 6 were written in by Bernard.

Of the 10 towns in Maine, 5 (Bowdoinham, Cape Elizabeth, Sanford, Topsham, and Windham) were by act, and named by Bernard; 1 (Bowdoinham), by act not signed by him; the other 4, not by act.

Of these 49 names, we find that the following 12 were given in honor of Americans: Belchertown, Shutesbury, Fitchburg, Royalston, Lanesborough, Williamstown, Hubbardstown, Worthington, *Bowdoinham*, *Gorham*, *Sanford*, and probably Templeton; 2 were Indian names, Natick and Marshpee; 2 Scriptural, Sharon and Lebanon; Ashfield, Newburyport, and Northborough probably originated here; Buxton was in honor of its first minister; Wellfleet and Ware are local corruptions; Becket, Ashby, *Topsham*, *Boothbay*, can hardly be traced; *Bristol* and *Cape Elizabeth* are revivals of old names.

We have thus accounted for 29 names; and the remaining 20 are referable, with almost entire certainty, to the peerage, or to English statesmen.

Governor Bernard himself is responsible for Bernardstown, Tyringham (which was the name of a family * he represented), and Shutesbury,

* Very little is known as to Governor Bernard's family.   It seems certain that these Bernards were settled at Abingdon, near Northampton, and that a certain Francis B. there

named for his wife's uncle, Governor Shute, as Barrington was for her cousin. Winchendon probably was owing to a family connection.

Pittsfield, Coleraine, Sandisfield, Athol, Ashburnham, Chesterfield, Warwick, Lenox, Granby, Shelburne, Conway, Winchendon, are all names to be found in the peerage. Wilbraham is evidently an English family name, — possibly that of some personal friend, as Paxton was.

THOMAS HUTCHINSON, 1769–1774.

During his administration there were incorporated in Massachusetts limits, 17 towns; 9 by act, of which he named 7. In Maine, 9 towns; 7 by act, all but one being written by Hutchinson.

Of these 26 towns, Cohasset is Indian; Northbridge, West Stock-bridge, West Springfield, and *New Gloucester* are evidently derived from other towns; *Hallowell, Princeton, Vassallborough,· Winslow, Winthrop,* Williamsburg, Partridgefield, *Pepperrellborough,* Huntington, *Waldoboro',* Leverett, are all derived from Americans; Norwich is named from the town in Connecticut; Alford, Southwick, and Ludlow are probably named from the first settlers or proprietors.

Westminster is evidently English; Mansfield, Gageborough, and Whately are the only names certainly given in honor of Englishmen.

List of Towns from 1732 to 1774.·

137. Harvard	June 29, 1732,	Act.
138. Sheffield	June 22, 1733,	Act.
139. Halifax ᵃ	July 4, 1734,	Act.
140. Tewkesbury . . .	Dec. 23, 1734,	Act.
141. Berkeley	April 18, 1735,	Act.
142. Grafton	do. do.	Act.
143. Upton	June 14, 1735,	Act.
144. Acton	July 3, 1735,	Act.
145. Waltham	Jan. 4, 1737–8,	Act.
146. Bolton	June 24, 1738,	Act.
147. Sturbridge . . .	do. do.	Act.
148. Chelsea.	Jan. 10, 1738–9,	Act.
149. Hardwick	do. do.	Act.

had three sons; of whom the second, Francis, was father of Sir Robert Bernard, of Huntington, created a baronet July 1, 1662. This branch became extinct, in 1789, in the person of the fifth baronet.

The third son of Francis Bernard first named was Thomas, great-grandfather of our Sir Francis. Our Governor was created a baronet, April 5, 1769, whose grandson, Sir Francis Bernard-Morland, is the present baronet.

There was, however, a different family named Bernard, using different arms, and set-tled at Castle Bernard. Of this family was Francis Bernard, who had three children: Francis, m. Lady Anne Petty, only child of Henry, Earl of Shelburne; Ludlow, whose grandson, Francis Bernard, was made Earl of Bandon; and Elizabeth, who married James Caulfield, second Viscount Charlemont. It will be noticed that Shelburne and Charlemont were among the names selected by Governor Bernard, though this may be but a coincidence.

ᵃ July 4, 1734, Litchfield was incorporated; and Jan. 6, 1732, Nottingham (now Hudson) was also made a town. These were both parts of Dunstable, and were both set off to New Hampshire. March 4, 1733-4, Rumford (now Concord) was incorporated by act; but this also was soon transferred to New Hampshire.

July 4, 1734, Somers was incorporated, being set off from Enfield. Both towns, as well as Suffield, were transferred to Connecticut.

150. Stockbridge ᵃ	. .	June 22, 1739,	Act.			
151. Wareham	. . .	July 10, 1739,	Act.			
152. Holden	. . . .	Jan. 9, 1739–40,	Act.			
153. Leominster	. . .	June 23, 1740,	Act.			
154. Western	. . . .	Jan. 16, 1740–1,	Act.			
155. Blandford	. . .	April 10, 1741,	Act.			
156. Pelham	. . . .	Jan. 15, 1741–2,	Act.			
157. Douglas	. . . .	1746.				
158. New Braintree	. .	Jan. 31, 1750–1.				
159. Palmer	. . . . .	Jan. 30; 1751–2,	Act.			
160. South Hampton	. .	Jan. 5, 1753, ᵇ	Act.			
161. Shirley	. . . .	Jan. 5, 1753.				
162. Spencer	. . .	April 3, 1753,	Act.			
163. Pepperrell	. . .	April 6, 1753,	Act.			
164. South Hadley	. .	April 12, 1753.				
165. Greenfield	. . .	June 9, 1753,	Act.			
166. New Salem	. . .	June 15, 1753.				
167. Montague	. . . .	Dec. 22, 1753.				
168. Granville	. . . .	Jan. 25, 1754,	Act.	Named possibly by Shirley		
169. Lincoln ᶜ	. . . .	April 19, 1754.				
170. Petersham	. . .	April 20, 1754,	Act.	do.	do.	do.
171. Greenwich	. . .	do. do.	Act.	do.	do.	do.
172. Charlton	. . . .	Nov. 2, 1754.				
173. Danvers	. . . .	June 16, 1757,	Act.			
174. Amherst	. . . .	Feb. 13, 1759,	Act.			
175. New Marlborough	.	June 15, 1759.				
176. Egremont	. . . .	Feb. 13, 1760,	Act.			
177. Monson	. . . . .	April 25, 1760.				
178. Pittsfield	. . . .	April 21, 1761,	Act.			
179. Great Barrington	.	June 30, 1761,	Act.			
180. Coleraine	. . . .	do. do.	Act.	By Bernard named.		
181. Belchertown	. . .	do. do.	Act.			
182. Shutesbury	. . .	do. do.	Act.			
183. Ware	. . . . .	Nov. 25, 1761,	Act.	do.	Bernard	do.
184. Sandesfield	. . .	March 6, 1762,	Act.	do.	Bernard	do.
185. Tyringham	. . .	do. do.	Act.	do.	Bernard	do.
186. Bernardstown	. .	do. do.	Act.	do.	Bernard	do.
187. Athol	. . . . .	do. do.	Act.	do.	Bernard	do.
188. Templeton	. . .	do. do.	Act.	do.	Bernard	do.
189. Chesterfield	. . .	June 11, 1762,	Act.	do.	Bernard	do.
190. Oakham	. . . .	do. do.	Act.	do.	Bernard	do.
191. Natick	. . . . .	Feb. 23, 1762,	Act.			
192. Warwick	. . . .	Feb. 17, 1763,	Act.	do.	Bernard	do.
193. Marshpee	. . . .	June 14, 1763,	Act.			
194. Wilbraham	. . .	June 15, 1763,	Act.	do.	Bernard	do.
195. Wellfleet	. . . .	June 16, 1763,	Act.	do.	Bernard	do.
196. Newburyport	. .	Jan. 28, 1764,	Act.	do.	Bernard	do.
197. Fitchburg	. . . .	Feb. 3, 1764,	Act.	do.	Bernard	do.
198. Winchendon	. .	June 14, 1764,	Act.	do.	Bernard	do.

11*. Brunswick	. . . .	Jan. 26, 1738–9,	Act.
12*. Newcastle	. . . . . .	June 19, 1753,	Act.
13*. Harpswell	. . . . . .	Jan. 25, 1758,	Act.
14*. Woolwich	. . . . . .	Oct 20, 1759.	
15*. Pownalborough	. . . .	Feb. 13, 1760,	Act.

ᵃ There was an act June 20, 1739, to incorporate Winchester, formerly called Arlington. It was in Hampshire County, but I cannot find its present representative.

ᵇ New style commences.

ᶜ 1754 Carlisle was set off as a precinct at the same date as Lincoln, but in 1757 it was reincorporated with Concord. A new town of the name has since been formed.

199. Paxton	Feb. 12, 1765,	Act.	By	Bernard named.
200. Royalston	Feb. 16, 1765.			
201. Ashburnham	Feb. 22, 1765,	Act.	do.	Bernard do.
202. Sharon	June 20, 1765.			
203. Becket	June 21, 1765,	Act.	do.	Bernard do.
204. Lanesborough	do. do.			
205. Richmont	June 21, 1765,	Act.	do.	Bernard do.
206. Williamstown	do. do.			
207. Ashfield	do. do.	Act.	do.	Bernard do.
208. Charlemont	do. do.	Act.	do.	Bernard do.
209. Murrayfield	Oct. 31, 1765,	Act.	do.	Bernard do.
210. Northborough	Jan. 24, 1766,	Act.	do.	Bernard do.
211. Lenox	Feb. 26, 1767,	Act.	do.	Bernard do.
212. Ashby	March 6, 1767,	Act.	do.	Bernard do.
213. Hubbardstown	June 13, 1767,	Act.	do.	Bernard do.
214. Conway	June 16, 1767.			
215. Granby	June 11, 1768,	Act.	do.	Bernard do.
216. Shelburne	June 21, 1768,	Act.	do.	Bernard do.
217. Worthington	June 30, 1768,	Act.		
218. Cohasset	April 26, 1770.			
219. Westminster	do. do.	Act.		
220. Mansfield	do. do.			
221. Southwick	Nov. 17, 1771,	Act.		
222. Whately	April 24, 1771.		do.	Hutchinson named.
223. Princeton	do. do.	Act.	do.	Hutchinson do.
224. Williamsburg	do. do.	Act.	do.	Hutchinson do.
225. Gageborough	July 2, 1771,	Act.	do.	Hutchinson do.
226. Partridgefield	July 4, 1771,	Act.	do.	Hutchinson do.
227. Northbridge	July 14, 1772,	Act.	do.	Hutchinson do.
228. Alford	Feb. 16, 1773,	Act.	do.	Hutchinson do.
229. Norwich	June 29, 1773.			
230. West Stockbridge	Feb. 23, 1774.			
231. West Springfield	do. do.	Act.		
232. Ludlow	Feb. 28, 1774,	Act.	do.	Hutchinson do.
233. Leverett	March 5, 1774,	Act.	do.	Hutchinson do.
234. Hutchinson	June, 1774.			

[See Pepperrellborough, No. 30*.]

16*. Windham	June 12. 1762,	Act. do.	Bernard	do.
17*. Buxton	July 14, 1762.			
18*. Bowdoinham	Sept. 18, 1762,	Act.		
19*. Topsham	Jan. 31, 1764,	Act. do.	Bernard	do.
20*. Gorham	Oct. 30, 1764.			
21*. Boothbay	Nov. 3, 1764,	Act. do.	Bernard	do.
22*. Bristol	June 18, 1765.			
23*. Cape Elizabeth	Nov. 1, 1765,	Act. do.	Bernard	do.
24*. Lebanon	June 25, 1767.			
25*. Sanford	Feb. 23, 1768,	Act. do.	Bernard	do.
26*. Hallowell	April 26, 1771,	Act. do.	Hutchinson	do.
27*. Vassallborough	do. do.	Act.		
28*. Winslow	do. do.	Act. do.	Hutchinson	do.
29*. Winthrop	do. do.			
31*. Belfast	June 22, 1773.			
32*. Waldoborough	June 29, 1773.			
33*. Edgecomb	March 5, 1774,	Act. do.	Hutchinson	do.
34*. New Gloucester	March 8, 1774.			
30*. Pepperrellborough	June 9, 1772.	{ Named by Bernard, by act June 9, 1762, as a district.		

In the following list I have given such information as I have in regard to each name. One thing seems very evident, that in selecting the names of Englishmen no system was followed. Neither the successive premiers as such, nor the chief members of their cabinets, were selected. The members of the Board of Trade and Plantations furnished but two names at most, and the great generals and admirals are equally ignored. How far the naming of towns in other colonies interfered with the selection of names for Massachusetts, it is impossible to state.

In conclusion, I desire to call attention to a very admirable list of the dates of incorporation of the towns in Massachusetts, prepared by Mr. George W. Chase, and published in the Abstract of the Census of Massachusetts for 1860, pp. 215–237.

Origin of Names given from 1694 to 1774.

89. *Tiverton*, 1694. A town in Tiverton Hundred, co. Devon, 14 miles north of Exeter.

90. *Harwich*, 1694. A seaport in co. Essex bears this name.

91. *Attleborough*, 1694. There is a market-town of this name in co. Norfolk, 15 miles from Norwich, which probably gave rise to our name. There is also a hamlet of the name in the parish of Nuneaton, co. Warwick.

92. *Framingham*, 1700. This seems to be a corruption of Framlingham, of which name we find a town in Suffolk, Eng., and also Framlingham-Earl and Framlingham-Pigot in Norfolk.

93. *Dracut*, 1701-2. Sewall writes in his Diary that sixteen of the Council sign an order for making Dracut a town. There are several places of a similar name in England; viz., Draycot-Orne and Draycot-Foliat in Wiltshire, Draycott-Moor in Berks, and Draycott-in-the-Moors, co. Stafford.

94. *Brookline*, 1705. Termed by Sewall often Brookland. Its first name was Muddy River, and this may fairly be ranked among descriptive names derived from the peculiarities of location.

95. *Plympton*, 1707. This town was originally the north-western parish of Plymouth. It undoubtedly took its name from one of the Plymptons (P. St. Mary and Earl's Plympton) in Devonshire, which are similarly near neighbors to Plymouth in England. The river Plym gives its name to all these towns or parishes.

96. *Truro*, 1707. This is the name of a market-town in Cornwall, considered the chief town in the county. It is at the head of Falmouth harbor.

97. *Norton*, 1711. It would be pleasant to think that this name was given in honor of Rev. John Norton, who preached for some months at Plymouth. It seems more probable, however, that it was derived from the position of the town, as the northerly part of Taunton, from which it was set off.

98. *Needham*, 1711. Originally a part of Dedham and adjoining Newton. If we can imagine that the name was compounded of the two (as occurred in Connecticut in the name Hadlyme), the requisite parts are here. There is a parish of Needham in Norfolk, Eng., and a town called Needham-Market, in Suffolk, on the river Orwell, 3 miles from Stow market; and one or the other was undoubtedly the original of our town name.

99. *Pembroke*, 1711-12. The town of this name in South Wales is at the mouth of the Bristol Channel, about opposite to Barnstaple. It was a place of some importance, and its castle was besieged and captured by Cromwell. Thomas Herbert, Earl of Pembroke and Montgomery, was at this date a member of the Privy Council.

100. *Dighton.* Named most probably in honor of Frances Dighton, wife of Richard Williams, one of the first settlers, and sister of the second wife of Governor Thomas Dudley. There is no place of the name in the British Gazetteer, and no better derivation has been suggested. I must state, however, that I have seen no evidence to show positively that these

ladies were named Dighton, although the statement is made in many histories.

101. *Abington*, 1712. There is a parish of the name in Northamptonshire, Eng., 2 miles from Northampton. Also Great and Little Abington in Cambridgeshire, 9 miles from Cambridge. The title of Earl of Abingdon was held by Montague Bertie in 1713 ; but the name is probably here derived from one of the above-cited parishes.

102. *Chatham*, 1712. The only place of the name in England is the famous seaport in Kent, the site of a royal dock-yard from Queen Elizabeth's time.

103. *Weston*, 1712–13. This was probably a name derived from its locality, it having been the extreme western portion of Watertown. Barber says that before its incorporation it had been called the westerly, more westerly, and most westerly precinct in Watertown. The name follows the analogy of its next neighbor, New Town or Newton.

104. *Lexington*, 1714. I have elsewhere discussed the reasons for giving the name to this town. On any theory, it was evidently derived from that of the parish of Lexington, Laxington, or Laxton, co. Nottingham, a village of some 650 inhabitants in 1841.

105. *Medway*, 1713. When this town was set off from Medfield, a souvenir of the first name was thus preserved in that of Medway, taken from that of the English river on which Chatham is situated.

106. *Leicester*, 1712–13. It is a fair surmise that this name was given in honor of Robert Dudley, Earl of Leicester, the famous favorite of Queen Elizabeth. Governor Joseph Dudley (as we learn from Draper's History of Spencer) was in 1686 owner of lands adjoining this settlement, and his sons Paul and William were proprietors of the new town in 1714. The others were chiefly residents of Roxbury and Boston ; and, as Dudley was then Governor, the naming of the town might well be given to him.

107. *Northfield*, 1713. Although there is a Northfield in Worcestershire, Eng., this town seems to have been named from its site. It was the most northern town in the colony, and it lies "on an elevated plain, rising above the meadows on the Connecticut." (Barber.)

108. *Rutland*, 1714. This is the name of a small county in England, bordering on Leicestershire. The title of Duke of Rutland was conferred on John Manners, ninth Earl, in 1703. He died Jan. 10th, 1710–11, and was succeeded by his son John, who married a daughter of the patriot William Lord Russell. This latter died Feb. 22, 1720–21 ; and, though he was in favor at the accession of George I., he was not of sufficient prominence to have been thus commemorated. I therefore feel inclined to give the origin of the name here to the county, and as very probably suggested by its proximity to Leicestershire.

9*. *Berwick, Maine*, 1713. We must regard this town as named after the city of Berwick-upon-Tweed. At this time there was the famous general James Fitz-James, illegitimate son of King James II., who was known by the title of Duke of Berwick. As he was at this time high in the service of France, it is of course impossible to suppose that our town was named for him.

109. *Chilmark*, 1714. This is a parish in Wiltshire, in the union of Tisbury. Of course, the name was given for the same reason as that of Tisbury (1671), which see.

110. *Sutton*, 1715. Of the family of this name in 1715 were Robert, Lord Lexington ; and also, in a junior branch, Sir Robert Sutton, K. B., a diplomatist, privy councillor (1722), and member of Parliament. Sutton is, however, a name of frequent occurrence in England, over sixty parishes of the name being given in the gazetteers. The probability is, therefore, that some one of these influenced the choice of the name of our town.

111. *Littleton*, 1715. Said by Barber to have been named, in 1715, in honor of Hon. George Lyttelton, M.P., and one of the Commissioners of the Treasury. But at that time the head of the family was Sir Charles L., who had been Governor of Jamaica, and who died May 2, 1716, aged 86. His son, Sir Thomas L., was M.P., &c., and died in 1751 ; being succeeded

by his eldest son, Sir George L., who was born in 1709. This last named was Chancellor of the Exchequer in 1755, and made Lord Lyttelton in 1757. The story seems, therefore, unfounded. It is rather probable that it derived its name from being a little town ; for, as Barber states, "it was formerly a gore of land, not included in any of the adjoining towns, and it remained in this state many years after they were incorporated."

112. *Hopkinton*, 1715. Named in honor of Edward Hopkins of London, who had been a settler at Hartford, and Governor of that colony. He returned to England, and by his will left a bequest of £500 to Harvard College. In 1713 this money was received, and " laid out in the purchase of an extensive tract of land, to which the name of Hopkinton was given, in honor of the donor." (Quincy's Hist. of Harv. Coll., i. 205.) The Court records also expressly state, when the petition was presented, that the village was to be incorporated " by the name of Hopkinton to the perpetuating the memory of the pious benefactor."

10*. *Georgetown, Maine,* 1716. Of course, in honor of the new King.

113. *Westborough,* 1717. Formerly part of Marlborough, and hence named. " The territory thus set off by the Act of the General Court, passed Nov. 19, 1717, was from its geographical position called Westborough." (Hudson's Hist. of Marlborough, p. 114.)

47. *Brookfield,* 1673–1718. This name, given to the revived settlement which had been broken up by the Indians, seems to be derived from the natural features of the locality. " There are large tracts of meadow and intervale upon Quabaog river, which runs in a westerly direction through the town." (Barber.) The abundance of water and plains in the town would account satisfactorily for the name. The revival of the township does not seem to have been a new creation, and the town claims precedence according to its original date.

114. *Sunderland,* 1718. A precinct before named Swampfield was incorporated as a town at this date. The name was undoubtedly given in honor of Charles Spencer, Earl of Sunderland, at this time prime minister. He married· a daughter of the Duke of Marlborough, and his descendants inherit that title.

115. *Bellingham,* 1719. At first a part of Dedham. Obviously named in honor of Governor Richard Bellingham ; whose family, however, was at that date extinct in this country.

116. *Holliston,* 1724. Named in honor of Thomas Hollis of London, the great benefactor of Harvard College, who died in 1731.

117. *Walpole,* 1724. In honor of Sir Robert Walpole, then Prime Minister.

118. *Methuen,* 1725. This is unquestionably a personal name. John Methuen negotiated in 1703 a treaty between England and Portugal, by which English woollen manufactures were to be admitted into Portugal ; and, in return, England agreed that the duty on wines from Portugal should always be less by one-third than those on wines from France. The Methuen treaty was therefore of great commercial importance, and must have had considerable influence on our trade, which was largely with Spain and Portugal. John Methuen had a son, Sir Paul M., of the Privy Council, 1714, Secretary of State, 1716, Ambassador to Spain, &c. A junior branch is represented by the Barons Methuen of Corsham, created in 1838.

119. *Stoneham,* 1725. Probably a descriptive name, as the "surface of the township is rather rocky and uneven." (Barber.) We note, however, that in Suffolk, Eng., are found Stonham-Aspel, Stonham-Earl, and Stonham-Parva.

120. *Easton,* 1725. Perhaps in honor of John Easton, Governor of Rhode Island, 1690–94, as was his father Nicholas E. before him. Bristol County adjoining Rhode Island, the magnates of the latter place were probably highly honored in the former.

121. *Kingston,* 1726. Probably a name given soon after the news of the death (March 5th, 1726) of Evelyn Pierrepont, first Duke of Kingston, who had

been Lord Privy Seal, and Lord President of the Council, 1716-1720. It may, however, be the antithesis of Provincetown.

122. *Stoughton*, 1726. Undoubtedly, in honor of William Stoughton, the Lieutenant-Governor, Chief Justice, &c., who died in 1701. His nephew, William Tailer, was Lieutenant-Governor before and after 1726, and at '. this time was member of the Council.

123. *Provincetown*, 1727. This town is the extreme end of Cape Cod, and was incorporated as the Province Town; the inhabitants being exempted from taxation.

124. *Hanover*, 1727. This name and that of Lunenburg were, of course, derived from the German possessions of the Royal family. June 11, 1727, was the commencement of the reign of George II., a fit time for such a naming; but the nearly coinciding of the dates is, of course, accidental.

125. *Uxbridge*, 1727. Henry Paget, Earl of Uxbridge, was at that time a member of the Privy Council.

126. *Southborough*, 1727. Formed from the south part of Marlborough, and thence named.

127. *Shrewsbury*, 1727. George Talbot, fourteenth Earl of Shrewsbury, and premier Earl of England, the wearer of the title at that time, succeeded, in 1718, his relative Charles, Duke of Shrewsbury. He was, I presume, a Roman Catholic, and seems not to have been in public life. The name was very probably in memory of the Duke, who had made a great figure in public life, and whose conversion to Protestantism was a famous event.

128. *Middleton*, 1728. At this date there 'were two peers; viz., Francis Willoughby, second Lord Middleton, who had served in Parliament, and Alan Brodrick, second Viscount Middleton, who was soon after one of the two Comptrollers of the accounts of the Army. It seems most likely, however, to have derived its name from its locality being, as Barber says, "formed of the united corners of several adjoining towns."

129. *Lunenburg*, 1728. See *Hanover*. The title of Elector of Brunswick. Lunenburg belonged to George I., and was commonly used.

130. *Bedford*, 1729. Wriothesley Russell, third Duke of Bedford, succeeded to the title in 1711, and died in 1732, aged 24 years. He was probably debarred by ill-health, as well as youth, from becoming prominent. His father was Lord High Constable, and member of the Privy Council; and his grandfather (second son of the first Duke) was the noted patriot, Lord William Russell. One family of the Russells of New England is descended from the same main stock, though long before it was ennobled.

131. *Westford*, 1729. Probably named from its locality being originally the *west* precinct of Chelmsford.

132. *Wilmington*, 1728. Spencer Compton, Lord Wilmington, was then member of the Privy Council. He was third son of the third Earl of Northampton, and died, unmarried, July 4, 1743. He was Speaker in 1714 and 1722, made Baron W. in 1728, Lord Privy Seal in 1730, and the same year was made Earl of W. The title of Baron W. was again granted to the ninth Earl of Northampton, and is borne by the present Earl.

133. *Raynham*, 1731. This was the name of the seat of Lord Townshend.

134. *Brimfield*, 1731. Originally set off from Springfield in 1701; and soon, says Barber, called by this name. We find in the gazetteer the parish of Brimpsfield, co. Gloucester, Eng., 8 miles from the city of Gloucester.

135. *Dudley*, 1731. This township was originally granted to Paul and William Dudley, sons of Governor Joseph Dudley. The name " was given to it as a token of respect to the above-mentioned men, who were principal proprietors of the soil, and great benefactors to the first settlers in their infancy," says Barber.

136. *Townshend*, 1732. Charles Townshend, Viscount Townshend, one of the Privy Council, Secretary of State, &c. He was brother-in-law of Sir Robert Walpole, and prominent in the political struggles of the time. The present Marquess Townshend is his representative.

137. *Harvard*, 1732.   Undoubtedly in honor of Rev. John Harvard, the founder of Harvard College.
138. *Sheffield*, 1733.   Edmund Sheffield, Duke of Buckinghamshire, succeeded in 1720, and died a minor in 1735.   His father, John, third Earl of Mulgrave, Marquess of Normanby, was made Duke of B. in 1703.   He was Lord Privy Seal, 1702, and Lord Chamberlain in 1710.   He was also a writer of some note in his time.   Although the claim to have given the name to our town seems weak, still it must be remembered that the now famous town of Sheffield has grown into importance in the present century, and had in 1733 no apparent claims for commemoration.
139. *Halifax*, 1734.   George Montague, first Earl of Halifax of the second creation, was nephew, and successor in the barony of Halifax, of Charles Montagu, the famous Chancellor of the Exchequer under William III. This Earl was a K. B., and member of the Privy Council, but not of great note.   His uncle, however, also Earl of Halifax, had made the title renowned.   This Earl married first Richarda-Posthuma, daughter of Richard Saltonstall of Chippen-Warden, co. Northampton, a branch of the family to which our Saltonstalls belong.   He died in 1739.
139a. Litchfield, Nottingham, Rumford, and Somers were named at this time. Somers and Nottingham were the titles of two of the greatest Lord Chancellors England had seen.   The barony of Somers became extinct in 1716, but the earldom of Nottingham still remains in the family of Finch.   The title of Earl of Litchfield was held in 1734 by George Henry Lee, of Ditchley.
   Rumford may well be a variation of Romford, the name of a parish in co. Essex, Eng.
140. *Tewksbury*, 1734.   This is the name of a town in Gloucestershire, Eng., famous for its Abbey.   It had been, however, one of the titles of George II., who was in 1706 made Baron Tewkesbury, Viscount Northallerton, Earl of Milford-Haven, Marquess and Duke of Cambridge.   In 1714, he became Prince of Wales; and, on his accession, in 1727, all his dignities merged in the Crown.   Still this use of the name is the most probable reason for its adoption here.
141. *Berkley*, 1735.   James Berkley, Earl of Berkeley, and William Berkeley, Lord Berkeley of Stratton, were both members of the Privy Council. Perhaps a better claim can be made for Dean Berkeley, who resided here from 1729 to 1731, and who was made Bishop of Cloyne in 1733.
142. *Grafton*, 1735.   Charles Fitz-Roy, Duke of Grafton, was member of the Privy Council.   He was a grandson of Charles II., and repeatedly held high offices.   He died May 6th, 1757.
143. *Upton*, 1735.   Origin unknown.   It may have been so named from some early proprietor.   In Ireland, at this period, there was a family of the name; of whom Clotworthy Upton, of Castle Upton, had a daughter, the Baroness Langford, and a nephew, Clotworthy Upton, created Baron Templetown in the peerage of Ireland in 1776.
144. *Acton*, 1735.   This name occurs in several counties in England, and we are at a loss to account for its application here.   There is a family of the name, baronets, of whom Sir Whitmore Acton died in 1732, and his son, Sir Richard, died in 1791; but I believe neither were prominent in public life.
11*. *Brunswick, Maine*, 1737.   A name proposed in 1714, says Williamson.   It was in honor of the new royal family.
145. *Waltham*, 1737.   There are several places of the name in England.   Perhaps the best claim can be made for Waltham-Abbey, co. Essex, Eng.; to which place belongs Nasing, the home of Rev. John Eliot, and other early settlers in New England.
146. *Bolton*, 1738.   Charles Powlet, third Duke of Bolton, was long a member of the Council, and high in office.   In 1733 he was out of favor at Court, but in 1740 was one of the Lords Justices during the King's absence. He died Aug. 26, 1754, aged 69 years.
147. *Sturbridge*, 1738.   Stourbridge, in Worcestershire, Eng., is a market-town: Sturbridge, or Stourbridge, is also the name of a hamlot 2 miles from

Cambridge, where an annual fair is held under the jurisdiction of the University.

148. *Chelsea*, 1738–39. The suburb of London thus named is chiefly noted for the hospital for superannuated soldiers. The name would naturally be well known here, and appropriately given to a village so near Boston, and situated on its harbor.

149. *Hardwicke*, 1738–39. Philip Yorke, Lord Hardwicke, was in 1733 made a peer, was of the Privy Council, and Chief Justice of the Court of King's Bench. In 1737 he was made Lord High Chancellor, an office he filled for nearly twenty years with the greatest credit. He died March 6th, 1764, aged 73.

Barber says of this town that before its incorporation it was known as Lambstown, from its first proprietor, Joshua Lamb.

150. *Stockbridge*, 1739. There is a market-town so named in Hampshire, 7 miles from Andover and 9 miles from Winchester. There was a family of this name in Massachusetts, and some member of it may have been interested in this settlement.

151. *Wareham*, 1739. There is a considerable market-town of this name in Dorsetshire, Eng.

152. *Holden*, 1740. "It was named," says Barber, "in honor of Hon. Samuel Holden, one of the Directors of the Bank of England, who was a generous benefactor to the literary and religious interests of the country. His donations amounted to £4,847 New England currency, and his widow and daughters farther contributed £5,585. With a part of the latter sum, Holden Chapel, in the University at Cambridge, Mass., was erected in 1745."

153. *Leominster*, 1740. This is the name of a large market-town in Herefordshire, Eng.

154. *Western*, 1740–41 (name changed to *Warren* in 1834). This may have been so named, as being the western part of Brookfield. It is in that case to be compared with Weston.

155. *Blandford*, 1741. Undoubtedly derived from the title of Marquess of Blandford, the second of the honors belonging to the Duke of Marlborough. In 1741 the bearer of the title was Charles Spencer, third Earl of Sunderland; who was the son of Anne, second daughter of the great Duke of Marlborough. His cousin William, Earl of Godolphin, son of the eldest daughter, died s. p. in 1731; and, in 1733, on the death of the mother, Spencer succeeded to the dukedom also. Holland (Hist. Western Mass., ii. 10) says that Governor Shirley came hither in a ship called the "Blandford," which circumstance would suggest the name to him.

156. *Pelham*, 1742. This is the well-known family name of Thomas, Duke of Newcastle, who, with his brother Henry Pelham, was almost supreme in English politics.

157. *Douglas*, 1746. This was the family name of James Douglas, sixth Duke of Hamilton, and of Archibald, Duke of Douglas. According to Barber, however, the town was named in honor of Dr. William Douglas, of Boston, one of the proprietors and a considerable benefactor of the town. He is best known as the author of a history of New England.

158. *New Braintree*, 1751. A name derived from the town already noted.

159. *Palmer*, 1752. Thomas Palmer was of our Council, and Chief Justice C. C. Pleas, Suffolk, from 1711 till his death in 1740. His son Thomas was a Mandamus Counsellor (but did not serve), and a benefactor to Harvard College.

160. *South Hampton*, 1753. This had been the south precinct of North Hampton.

12*. *Newcastle, Maine*, 1753. In honor of the Duke of Newcastle, then and for many years one of the most noted of English politicians.

161. *Shirley*, 1753. Of course, in honor of Governor William Shirley.

162. *Spencer*, 1753. Possibly a name given by the Lieutenant-Governor (then acting Governor) *Spencer* Phips. He was the adopted son of Sir William Phips, being Spencer Bennett, nephew of Lady Phips, who was daughter of Roger Spencer. The well-known title of Earl Spencer was created

in 1765; but in 1753 Charles Spencer, third Earl of Sunderland, had succeeded to the honors of his maternal grandfather, and was the second
Duke of Marlborough. The high position of the Duke in political
life inclines us to the belief that the town was named in his honor.

163. *Pepperrell*, 1753. In honor of Sir William Pepperrell.

164. *South Hadley*, 1753. The south part of Hadley.

165. *Greenfield*, 1753.. Named from its locality, being an extensive field, and situated on Green River. It was part of Deerfield.

166. *New Salem*, 1753. Derived from Salem, of course.

167. *Montague*, 1753. Of this name were the Montagus, Dukes of Montagu, of
whom the second Duke died s. p. m. in 1749, having been a member of
the administration for several years, Master General of the Ordnance,
&c. ; and also the Earls of Sandwich. The fourth Earl was of the Privy
Council, First Lord of the Admiralty, Minister to the Congress at Aix-
la-Chapelle, &c. His brother William was Captain of the "Mermaid"
at the taking of Cape Breton. Of a junior branch was Edward Wortley-Montagu, whose wife was the famous Lady Mary Wortley-Montagu.
I cannot doubt that Captain Montague, who was with Pepperrell, and who
was sent home to carry the news of the victory at Louisburg, was the
person honored by this selection of a name.

168. *Granville*, 1754. John Carteret, Earl Granville, was Lord President of the
Privy Council, and well known in the annals of the State. The title be-
came extinct at the death of his son, in 1776 ; but has been revived in the
Leveson-Gower family, in 1833.

169. *Lincoln*, 1754. Henry Clinton, ninth Earl of Lincoln, held various high
offices. He was closely allied with the all-powerful Pelhams, his mother
being the sister, and his wife the daughter, of Henry Pelham. In 1768,
he succeeded his uncle, Thomas Pelham, as Duke of Newcastle.

169a, 1754. *Carlisle* may have been so named for the city ; but more probably it
was in honor of one of the Earls of Carlisle, of the Howard family. At
this date the possessor of the title was Henry, fourth Earl, who was not
of much note ; but his father, Charles, had played an important part in
politics.

170. *Petersham*, 1754 This is the second title of the Earls of Harrington. William Stanhope, Lord President of the Council, was, in 1742, made Viscount
Petersham and Earl of Harrington. He was distinguished in political
life, and died in 1756.

171. *Greenwich*, 1754. The suburb of London thus named is famous for the Royal
Hospital for seamen.

172. *Charlton*, 1754. There are many places of this name in England. As a
family name it was borne by Sir Francis Charlton, Bart., who was Gen-
tleman of the Privy Chamber, Receiver-General of the Post-office in
1755, &c. The Howards, Earls of Suffolk, are also Barons Howard of
Charlton. In 1754, the title was borne by Henry Bowes Howard, eleventh
Earl, who was deputy Earl Marshal.

173. *Danvers*, 1757. There is, I believe, no locality of this name in England.
There are two families of baronets named D'Anvers, but I think it more
probable that the person honored was Sir Danvers Osborn, Bart., Governor of New York in 1753, whose secretary Pownall had been. Sir Danvers was grandson of Sir John Osborn, whose mother was Eleanor
Danvers, and whose grandmother was Dorothy Danvers, both ladies of
the family of the name settled at Dauntsey, co. Wilts. Yet it must be
said that the name was given to it as a district, Jan. 28, 1752, in an act
signed by Phips ; and the town was incorporated June 16, 1757 ; while
Pownall did not arrive here till August 2, and this act was signed by the
Council. Sir Danvers Osborn was made Governor of New York, June
6, 1753. He married Mary, sister of George Montague-Dunk, second Earl
of Halifax, who was President of the Board of Trade, 1748–60. Another
sister married Joseph Jekyll ; a relative, probably, of John Jekyll, of
Boston, Collector of Customs. I still think that this name must be connected with Sir Danvers Osborn.

13*. *Harpswell, Maine*, 1758.   This name was proposed in 1714, says Williamson.   There is a parish of the name in co. Lincoln, Eng.
174. *Amherst*, 1759.   In honor of Jeffrey, Lord Amherst, then Commander-in-
Chief of the forces in the French War.   Louisburg was taken July 26,
1758 ; Ticonderoga, Crown Point, and Quebec, in 1759.
14*. *Woolwich, Maine*, 1759.   The famous military and naval depot in England
is 9 miles from London.
175. *New Marlborough*, 1759.   See *Marlborough.*
176. *Egremont*, 1760.   Charles Wyndham, Earl of Egremont, was of the Privy
Council, &c.   In 1761 he was made Secretary of State on the resignation
of William Pitt.
177. *Monson*, 1760.   John Monson, second Lord Monson, succeeded his father in
1748.   The first Lord was for many years first Lord Commissioner of
Trade and Plantations.
15*. *Pownalborough, Maine*, 1760.   In honor of Governor Thomas Pownall.
178. *Pittsfield*, 1761.   Of course, in honor of William Pitt, Lord Chatham.
179. *Great Barrington*, 1761.   Named probably for William Barrington, Viscount
Barrington, who was of the Privy Council, Secretary at War, Chancellor
of the Exchequer, &c.   His family name was Shute, and he was nephew
of Governor Samuel Shute, of Mass.   The prefix " Great " was to distin-
guish this town from the one in Bristol County, now a part of Rhode
Island.   He was own cousin to Bernard's wife ; she being Amelia,
daughter of Stephen Offley and Anne Shute.
180. *Coleraine*, 1761.   Gabriel Hanger, or Aungier, was created Baron Coleraine
in the peerage of Ireland, Dec. 1, 1761.
181. *Belchertown*, 1761.   In honor of Governor Jonathan Belcher, who was one
of the principal proprietors at its first granting.
182. *Shutesbury*, 1761.   In memory, doubtless, of Governor Samuel Shute, who
was uncle to Governor Bernard's wife.
183. *Ware*, 1761.   Holland, ii. 286, says that the town was named from the river
on which it stands ; and that again was derived from the *weirs*, or *wears*,
constructed in the river to aid in taking salmon.
184 *Sandisfield*, 1761?   Clearly in honor of Samuel Sandys, Lord Sandys, who
was a member of the Privy Council, and in 1761 made first Lord of
Trade and the Plantations.
185. *Tyringham*, 1762.   Tyringham with Tilgrove is the name of a parish in
Buckinghamshire, 4 miles from Olney.   Barber says that our town was
so named at the suggestion of Viscount Howe, who passed through the
place a few days before he was killed at Ticonderoga, July 6, 1758, and
who owned property in the English village.   But the true solution is probably that Governor Bernard was the descendant, and in 1770 became the
representative, of the family of Tyringham, as Burke's Baronetage shows,
under the title Morland.
186. *Bernardston*, 1762.   Presumably in honor of Sir Francis Bernard, Governor
of the Province from 1760 till 1769.
187. *Athol*, 1762.   James Murray, second Duke of Athol, was a representative
peer, Privy Councillor, 1734, and Lord Privy Seal of Scotland.   He died
Jan. 8, 1764.
188. *Templeton*, 1762.   Richard Grenville, Earl Temple, brother-in-law of Pitt,
was a prominent member of the government at this date.   The American
branch of the family was then represented by John Temple, afterwards a
baronet.
189. *Chesterfield*, 1762.   Philip Dormer Stanhope, fourth Earl of Chesterfield, is
too well known to require comment.   He died March 24, 1773.
190. *Oakham*, 1762.   I presume that this refers to Oakhampton, co. Devon ; a
borough which Pitt represented in 1756, and which had also been represented by his father and his older brother.
191. *Natick*, 1762.   An Indian name.
16*. *Windham, Maine*, 1762.   This was the family name of the Earls of Egremont.   See No. 176.
17*. *Buxton, Maine*, 1762.   " It was so called " (says Williamson, ii. 366) " at
the instance of the Rev. ('Dr. Paul') Coffin, who originated from a

town of the same name in England." This is partly an error, as Paul was born in Newbury, Mass., son of Colonel Joseph C., who was great grandson of Tristram Coffin, the emigrant. This Tristram was grandson of "Nicholas Coffin of *Burton*, co. Devon." (See Memoir of Rev. Paul Coffin, Portland, 1855.) Here, again, is an error, the place being really *Brixton* : but I think it evident that Paul Coffin meant to refer to his ancestor's birthplace ; and, misled by some written authority, gave the present name, ri and u being easily confounded.

18*. *Bowdoinham, Maine*, 1762. In honor of the well-known family of Bowdoin. William Bowdoin was the owner, under a title from the Plymouth proprietors. (Williamson, ii. 367.)

192. *Warwick*, 1763. Francis Greville, eighth Lord Brooke, created Earl Brooke 1749, Knight of the Thistle 1753, made Earl of Warwick Nov. 27, 1759.

193. *Marshpee*, 1763. An Indian name.

194. *Wilbraham*, 1763. There is a family of the name of good position in Cheshire. (See Burke's Commoners, i. 315.) Holland, ii. 156, says that, in a memoir written by the son of the first pastor, it is stated that "the name (of Wilbraham) was very grievous to the then inhabitants ; and we can hardly be reconciled to it yet."

195. *Wellfleet*, 1763. The suggestion that I can quite confidently make is, that this is a corruption of *Whale-fleet*, — a phrase still in common use on the sea coast for the whaling fleet. Freeman (Hist. Cape Cod, ii. 655) says, " The whaling business was in early times carried on extensively here." This fishery, once the chief employment, was lucrative." The name was written in by Governor Bernard, who had first written the name of *Melton*, and had struck it out, probably thinking it too much like Milton.

196. *Newbury Port*, 1764. Origin evident.

19*. *Topsham, Maine*, 1764. There is a seaport of this name in Devonshire, Eng.

197. *Fitchburg*, 1764. Named in honor of John Fitch, one of the committee to obtain the act of incorporation. (See Barber, p. 566.)

198. *Winchendon*, 1764. Named undoubtedly by Governor Bernard, who was the eventual heir of the Tyringhams of Upper Winchendon. In an earlier generation, one of the Tyringhams married a Goodwyn ; and her cousin married the fourth Baron Wharton, whose son was made, in 1706, Viscount Winchenden and Earl of Wharton. The title became extinct, in 1731, in the person of the Duke of Wharton.

20*. *Gorham, Maine*, 1764. It was so named out of respect to Captain John Gorham, one of the early proprietors.

21*. *Boothbay, Maine*, 1764. Origin unknown.

199. *Paxton*, 1765. Charles Paxton was one of the Commissioners of Customs at Boston, was a refugee, &c.

200. *Royalston*, 1765. Named in honor of Colonel Isaac Royal, of Medford, one of the original proprietors. (Barber, p. 600.)

201. *Ashburnham*, 1765. John Ashburnham, second Earl of Ashburnham, was keeper of Hyde Park in 1753 ; and, July 12, 1765, was made Master of the Wardrobe and a Privy Councillor. This was some months after the town was named.

202. *Sharon*, 1765. A Scriptural name.

22*. *Bristol, Maine*, 1765. The old town of Bristol, Mass., had been set off to Rhode Island some twenty years before.

203. *Becket*, 1765. Unknown.

204. *Lanesborough*, 1765. I cannot find that any American of the name of Lane was concerned in this settlement. In 1751, George Fox, whose father married the sister and heiress of James Lane, Viscount Lanesborough in the peerage of Ireland, assumed the name and arms of Lane. In 1762, George Fox-Lane, having married the only child of Robert Benson, Lord Bingley, was created Baron Bingley. This peerage ended with his son Robert, who died s. p. ; but his nephew was the ancestor of the present Lord Conyers. The family is one of great wealth and importance.

205. *Richmont*, 1765. The seat of the Earl of Shelburne, first Commissioner of

Trade and Plantations, was Richmond Hill, co. Surrey. But more probably it was named for Charles Lennox, Duke of Richmond, who was
made a Privy Councillor Oct. 23, 1765, and principal Secretary of State
in 1766.
206. *Williamstown*, 1765. Named in honor of Colonel Ephraim Williams, Jr.,
founder of Williams College. (Barber, p. 105.)
207. *Ashfield*, 1765. It is worth noticing, that Lord Chancellor Thurlow was
created, in 1778, Lord Thurlow of Ashfield. He was King's Counsel in
1761, Solicitor-General in 1770, Attorney-General in 1771. His father
was rector of Ashfield in Suffolk. Still the name may be but a descriptive one.
208. *Charlemont*, 1765. James Caulfield, third Viscount Charlemont, married
Elizabeth, only daughter of Francis Bernard of Castle Mahon, co. Cork;
and had a son, James, who was, Oct. 29, 1763, created Earl of Charle-
mount, or Charlemont.
209. *Murrayfield*, 1765. In honor, doubtless, of William Murray, Lord Mansfield. At this date, he was Chief Justice of the Court of King's Bench
and a Privy Councillor.
The name was changed to Chester, 21 Feb. 1783.
23*. *Cape Elizabeth, Maine*, 1765. An old name, given first by Captain John
Smith, and never disused.
210. *Northborough*, 1766. The northern part of Westborough, which latter was
set off from Marlborough.
211. *Lenox*, 1767. This is the family name of the Duke of Richmond, who is
also Duke of Lennox and Baron Methuen in the peerage of Scotland.
He was at this date a Secretary of State.
212. *Ashby*, 1767. Possibly in honor of Francis, tenth Earl of Huntington, of the
Privy Council in 1760, who died in 1790. His oldest title was Baron
Hastings of Ashby de la Zouche, and Ashby was long the family seat.
213. *Hubbardstown*, 1767. " So called to perpetuate the name and memory of
Hon. Thomas Hubbard, of Boston, who was a large proprietor of lands
in this place." (Barber, p. 573.)
214. *Conway*, 1767. Henry Seymour Conway was one of the principal Secretaries of State from July 19, 1765, to Jan. 20, 1768.
24*. *Lebanon, Maine*, 1767. Scriptural.
25*. *Sandford, Maine*, 1767. Named in honor of Peleg Sandford, the proprietor
of this grant.
215. *Granby*, 1768. John, Marquess of Granby, afterwards Duke of Rutland, was
Master-General of the Ordnance from 1763 to 1772, and so a member of
the Cabinet.
216. *Shelburne*, 1768. William Fitz-Maurice, second Earl of Shelburne, of the new
creation, was one of the Secretaries of State from 1766 (succeeding the
Duke of Richmond) to November, 1768. In 1782, he became Prime Minister, and in 1784 was created Marquess of Lansdowne. His father, Charles,
was the fifth son of Thomas F.-M., twenty-first Baron of Kerry, first
Earl of Kerry, who married the sister of Henry Petty, last Earl of Shelburne. Charles, being the heir by his uncle's will, was created Earl of
Shelburne in 1753, and died in 1761.
217. *Worthington*, 1768. Colonel John Worthington was a member of the Council,
1767-68, and was one of the proprietors of this township. " His liberal-
ity " (says Holland, ii. 303) " to the settlers in building them a church
and grist mill at his own expense, and in assigning generous lots for min-
isterial and school purposes, well earned the distinction."
218. *Cohasset*, 1770. An Indian name.
219. *Westminster*, 1770. The English original is well known as one of the seven
boroughs of London. It seems to have been made a district by act, Oct.
20, 1759.
220. *Mansfield*, 1770. Lord Mansfield was Lord Chief Justice of England from
1756 to 1788. He died March 20, 1793.
221. *Southwick*, 1771. Origin unknown. There has been a family of the name
in New England. It may also be noted, that Southwark is, like Westminster, an integral part of London.

222. *Whately*, 1771.   Named by Hutchinson in honor of his friend, Thomas
     Whately, a member of the Board of Trade.   (See Hutchinson's letter to
     this effect, in Marvin's History of the town, p. 86.)
223. *Princeton*, 1771.   Named in honor of Rev. Thomas Prince, the Annalist,
     who was a large proprietor of this tract of land.   (Barber, p. 598.)
224. *Williamsburg*, 1771.   Named, undoubtedly, for some member of the influen-
     tial family resident in the neighboring town of Deerfield.
26*. *Hallowell, Maine*, 1771.
27*. *Vassallborough, Maine*, 1771.
28*. *Winslow, Maine*, 1771.
29*. *Winthrop, Maine*, 1771.
     All of these names are commemorative of distinguished American families.
225. *Gageborough*, 1771.   Of course, in honor of General Gage.   "Jan. 9, 1777, the
     people of the town petitioned to be called Cheshire, ' because the present
     name of Gageborough may serve to perpetuate the memory of the de-
     tested General Gage.' "   (Holland, Hist. of Western Mass., ii. 616.)   In
     1778, however, the name was changed to Windsor, by which it is still
     known.
226. *Partridgefield*, 1771.   Name changed to Peru, June 19, 1806.   It was named
     for Oliver Partridge, one of its former owners.
30*. *Pepperellborough, Maine*, 1771.   In honor of the well-known family.
227. *Northbridge*, 1772.   Said by Barber, p. 591, to have been "chiefly taken from
     Uxbridge, and derived its name from its situation and bearing relative to
     that town."
228. *Alford*, 1773.   Presumably in honor of Hon. John Alford, of Charlestown,
     who died Sept. 30, 1761, and who gave largely to charities.   He founded
     in this way the Professorship of Natural Theology at Harvard College.
     Hutchinson had advised in the settlement of the estate.
31*. *Belfast, Maine*, 1773.   "So called by request of an early settler, out of re-
     spect for the name of his native place in Ireland," says Williamson, ii.
     398.   The Scotch-Irish immigration was as late as about 1720.
229. *Norwich*, 1773.   It was settled by emigrants from Norwich, Conn.   In 1855
     the name was changed to Huntington, in honor of Charles P. Huntington,
     of Northampton.   (Holland, Hist. of Western Mass., ii. 238–9.)
230. *West Stockbridge*, 1774.
231. *West Springfield*, 1774.
     The origin of these names is evident.
232. *Ludlow*, 1774.   Origin unknown.   Roger Ludlow was one of the early set-
     tlers in Massachusetts, Deputy Governor in 1634, &c.; but he left no heirs.
     Edmund Ludlow was the well-known regicide.   Besides these personal
     names, Ludlow is the name of a town and famous castle in Shropshire.
33*. *Edgecomb, Maine*, 1774.   "Given by the General Court in honor of Lord
     Edgecomb, who was, at this crisis of political affairs, a distinguished friend
     to the interests of the Colonies." (Williamson, ii. 405.)   The Edgecombs
     had hereditary claims on Maine, having had a grant there in 1637.
34*. *New Gloucester, Maine*, 1774.   Granted in 1735 to the inhabitants of Glou-
     cester, Mass. (Williamson, ii. 406.)
233. *Leverett*, 1774.   In honor of the distinguished family of the name here.
234. *Hutchinson*, 1774.   In Worcester County, and named of course for the Gov-
     ernor.   In November, 1776, the name was changed to Barré, in honor of
     the distinguished advocate of Colonial rights in Parliament.

The President communicated a number of manuscript news-
letters of early date for publication in the " Proceedings,"—
one of them of the *annus mirabilis* 1666.

An extract of a Letter frō Cambridge: Dat: Apr.¹ 4ᵗʰ 66.

Here have arrived noe Shipes from Engld this winter, only one
from yᵉ west part of Engld, where yᵉ Sicknesse was nott yⁿ. Butt it

brought noe News frõm Londõ, soe y^t ye news wch is, is come from
other places & theirfore nott much nor certaine; Butt some there is
(viz) y^t ye plauge is Greatly ceast; though y^r is an after Report y^t itt
was encreased in London againe, by reason of ye Citize[ns] returing,
soe y^t ye abateing of itt was rather for want of subjec[ts] to work on
y^n any other thing.   Their hath been noe other Engagment of ye English & Dutch fleet, ye Dutch declining itt what they can, either outt of
policy or feare.   only ye Privaters have taken Merchant Shipes enough
to maintaine y^r wars allmost: Warre is proclaimed betweco Engld &
France soe y^t now y^r are.   3. Nations against 3. ye english, Spanish
& Sweads, against ye Dutch, danes and French: here is a report y^t y^e
King of France is stabd.
     Their is a strict act of parliament come forth against Nonconformists,
& is to be in force ye 25th of March, ye same day y^t ye prophesies of y^e
witneses rising is.   Admiral Mountague is in ye Tower who would
not fight wth his Squadron; ye cause of ye Loss of a compleat victory,
and Munck in his place.   20 Saile of dutch Shipes are gon outt to doe
what mischeife they can to ye english plantations in America: & wee
hear y^t Coll. Cartwright is Gott to Engld.   Three Shipes are prepar-
ing for N Engld:

An other Extract of a Letter Apr^{il} 11th 66 from Boston.

for News wee have little, only Mr Harwood writes 25th Jã: y^t peirce
& Clark were to come for New Egld in March: frõ Bilboa is advised
a League Between E: & Spain, offensive and defensive.   Engld:
Spain, portugall, ye Emperour, Bishop of Munster, Duke of Branden-
burg, & Swead unite against France, Holland and ye Dean, soe y^t in
appearance this Summer will bee a time of Great action in Europe,
and to be feared America will feel ye smart of it.
     m^r Kuowles hath lost 4 of his Childrē.

                         For the Honoured
                         Governo^r JOHN WINTHROP
                         Esqe at his house
                                        in Hartford
     Indorsed, — Copy of Letter of News.

     Now I shall tell you how matters stands as to the publiq^e affaires;
the Dutch coming the 4th May towards the Downs, where then the
Duke of Yorke lay with most the English fleete, reddy to saile to ports-
mouth to meet the French fleete, who were then arrived there, hee being
advised of their approach, made away for portsmoth, they missing butt
little of him come to an Ancher in Dover Roads, where they Ridd some
daies, and then came before this river, where they sent in a Squadron,
and drive from the boy of the Noer 10 saile of the King's shipps vnder
Shernes fort, fyring vpon each other all the while, and after that stood
out againe to their fleete, the wind being all the while easterly, the Duke
and French could nott come vppe vntell the 19th; that the fleetes got
sight of one another and soe moer time after, butt engaged nott, the
Duke coming to an Ancher in Soules Bay, where lying vntell the 28th;
that the Dutch came to him there with an easterly wind, and fought

both very fearce from 7 of the clock in the Morning vntell after sunn sett att Night, wherein severall of the best shipps in both fleetes were much torne and disabled, many Kild and wounded, far moer then either doe Own, for itt is Knowen that some shipps lost halfe their Men, and others very Many, both claimed the victory att First, and supposed to haue moer advantage vpon the other, then after vpon due examinaçon is found, butt that the losses are pretty equall, and the Dutch wright of itt that they had burnt the Admirall of the Blew Flagg, and Another, and sank some, besides the Royall Katherine, and Henry taken, butt lost againe, disabled the Duke of Yorkes Two shipps hee was in; that hee was Forst to goe over in the third, and that they lost butt One shipp in the fight, being taken, and another next morning by carelesnes of their own powder, butt the printed relation here saith otherwaies, and that moer are sank and burnt; whatever itt is the slaughter and Destruction hath been great on both sides, and neither haue cause of rejoyceing over the other, butt rather lament that soe much Christian Blood is shed between Two soe neere neighbours; next day after the Fight they were going to engage againe butt were prevented by a fogg or Mist, the Duke haueing the weather gage all day, and towards night the wind rose, they parted without doing moer Mischeaf to One the other, the Duke returning to Soale bay, and soe to the boy of the Noer, where now both English & French lie, the Dutch kept sea longer, went into Scotland, and came out againe, haueing been mett of att sea of Yarmoth, standing in for the texell, as is reported, butt that is yett vncertaine; Jf the Dutch did fight pretty well att sea, they haue nott the luck to doe soe att land; the French Armies, and of the Bishopp of Munsters take all befoer them, soe that if the King of France proceed On soe fast, hee will soone subdue them, haueing in few daies taken the well fortefyed Garrison Towns of Wesel, Orsoy, Reynberk, burick, Rees and Emmerick, and is said to bee befoer Deventer, that Nimegen is alsoe surrendred to him, with the strong Town of the Graue, and that Schenckenscans was assalted, and supposed to bee taken alsoe, An Invinceable strength lying vpon a point of an Island att the parting or deviding of Two great rivers, soe that itt seemes nothing can withstand him, haueing severall great Armies, Assaults many places att Once, and where hee finds the strongest Opposition, hee drawes them p'sently together, and forces them with main strength, sparing noe men nor mony neither, as is supposed; the Bishopp of Munster, that Jnstrument of Evill, has taken the strong towns of Groll, Dedensow, burcle, and others and is said to haue besedged Swoll, Butt the worst newes of all is, that the King of France haueing in hast made A Bridge over the River waell, came suddenly, and vnexpected to Arenem, and tooke itt p'sently; And soe is said to bee marched for Vytright, which is doubted may be taken befoer this time: And from thence proceed to Amsterdam, where they say they pull down all the outhouses about the Town, and that the States are come to sitt there, haueing left the Hague, being an open place; if the Towns in the low lands bee not better defended, the[n] the vpper Fronteir Garrisons haue been, itt will nott bee this sumers worke to subdue all; and truely many are afraid of itt, J cannott deny itt very much troubles mee.

Two Dutch Ambassadors are come over, and stay att Hampton Court vntell the King has Answer from the King of France, to whom hee has sent the Lord Hollyfax about itt, the Dutch fleete is out befoer the River, of an on, and said to bee 180 saile in all.

LONDON, 17ᵗʰ June, 1672.

PHILADELPHIA, June yᵉ 5ᵗʰ 1699.

About yᵉ Middle of Last Week a Sloop, belonging to this place, arrived from Carrolina, brought in wᵗʰ yᵐ two Priveteers that Came Last from Madagascar.   One of wᶜʰ went out Capᵗ Kidds Doctor from New york, but left Kidds Vessell many months since at Madagascar, They were both Taken and sent to prison yᵉ Same night they Came vp, and their mony secur'd ; two more were Taken at New Castle who had Taken passage on board Capᵗ Codman for New England, and their mony Seized, The Sloop that brought yᵐ is also Seiz'd.

They wᵗʰ a great many more Came passengers from Madagascar wᵗʰ one Capᵗ Shelly belonging to N: York, Severall of yᵐ are desperss'd about our Bay, especially about Cape May. Governᵗ Bass, & Capᵗ Snead, who is Deputy Judge of yᵉ Court of Admiralty, are gone Down in a Sloop wᵗʰ Expectation of taking them.   The Privateers have made great shares of mony.   Capᵗ Shelly plys of and on, expecting Vessells from New york.   A Messengᵗ sent from Cape May for N: York wᵗʰ Lettᵐ to Shellys owners (as is said) vpon advice was persued & Taken, and his Lettᵗ Taken and open'd, and he Secured at Burlington, the Lettᵗ forwarded by an Express to Govᵗ Bass.

Tis said Mᵗ Graverodd has Severall on board his Sloop for Verginia.

Last night wee have Advice of a Pink Arrived at New Castle from Barbadᵗ 4 weeks passage. I have not the Letters from her yett. I Send for yᵐ to-day. Shee is to Tarry some days at New Castle. As they Came wᵗʰ in our Capes a Sloop Came vp wᵗʰ yᵐ. Sayld Round yᵐ, ask yᵐ some Questions, yⁿ went off and Came to Anchor at the Horchills, they had about 50 men on board.   They are some have made a Voyage and wants to Come in, there Capᵗ name is Davis, Some on Board the Pink knew him.

BOSTON, June yᵉ 19, 1699.

Last thursday Captᵗ Kid came into Road Island harber ; yᵉ Governour sent yᵉ Collector in a boat wᵗʰ about 30 men well armed in order to goe on board, but Kid shot 2 great Guns, wᶜʰ caused yᵉ Collector to retreat.   Kids Sloope has 10. Guns, 8. Patteraroes. I shall be able to give a further accoᵗ by yᵉ next.

tis Governour Bass Jntercepted the letter to Shelleys Owner & broke itt Open, as itt is said in New Yorke.

NEW YORKE, April 29ᵗʰ 1700.

I am thankfull for yours of the 22ᵈ Instant, and what News is here, is contained in the following accᵒⁿ.

From Philadelf. we have advice, that 2 ships From London and one From Bristoll, are arrived there, but bring no News.

on Sattarday Last the Newport from Sandyhooke a crusing & Capᵗ Simmons for London ; Capᵗ Gill will saill for London tomorrow or next day & Cap! Bond in 10 or 12 Days; Cap! Keeler has Bills for London.

on Satterday arrived Phillidelphia Post, w' whom Came Coll. Quarry & The Deputy Shereffe, who brought w' him one Brown, Co!! Markham Son-in-Law, he was one of Emrys men, as itt was Said and goes home w' y° Rest.

Yesterday arrived a Barguentine from y° Bay of Compechy. John Trimingham master, 30 Days passage, he informs y' Bermudos Sloops wer taken by a pyrate Comming out of y° Bay in Sight of him, y' Last week about thirty Leagus off y° Capes of Virginia he saw a ship att Sea Desabled, and Comming up w' her found She was a ship of about 150 tuns, bound from Leverpoole to Virginia, who had been taken by a Pyrate on Sunday y° 20ᵗʰ Instant, y° master of y° Ship Informed Trimingham y' y° pyrate is a ship of 24 Gunns & 150 men, y' 3 days befor he was taken a pinke bound from London to Virginia which pinke they maned w' fifty men and take this Leverpool Ship and after they had plundered of what they Pleased they Cutt down all his masts & bolt Split and so Left him; when Trimingham mett him they had made mastes of ther yards and top masts & now standing in for Virginia; y° Pyrate Carryd away y° Carpenter and one man more, but who Commands this pyrat they cannot Lern, y° Saim pyrat had likwise taken a New England Sloop of six Guns.

BOSTON, May y° 6, 1700.

The above is a Coppy of a News Letter I had by y° Last post. No News offers hear, Cap! Rugells from Meves arived hear yesterday.

BOSTON, May y° 28, 1700.

HONᵇˡᵉ S⸱, — The Last Tuseday Cap! Green arived here, 8 weeks passage from London & 6 weeks from Cows. y° same day arived a Ship, 5 weeks passage from Plimoth, Cap! —— Comander, brings news y' y° advice man of war was arived in 3 weeks at Bristol wᵗʰ Cap! Kidd & all y° Prisoners y' went home wᵗʰ Cap! Wine; it is reported y' y° Parliament has petissioned y° King to putt of Cap! Kids Triall till y° next Sessions of Parlem!

There is warr Proclaimed between Denmark & Sweden. All mattʳˢ are quiet at home. 'Tis reported y° King Designes for Scotland. The King of Spain is well by y° Last advice.

Last Saturday arived here Cap! Morris in y° Newport wᵗʰ y° Prisnors from New-York.

Admirall Benbo intends to Saile for London this week. There is Severall vessels arived from Madera, Fiall & y° west Indes.

Cap! Robison Came out of London wᵗʰ Cap! Green & is dayly expected here. Cap! Jeffery was bound for New York about y° Same time.

Advice from New York y° Last post of y° misfortune at Callidonia, Viz. Cap! Campbel, one of y° Councel, who arived Last thursday, Saith y' he arived 8 dayes before y° Spanish blocked up y° port at Callidonia. 3 days after his arival he Comanded a parte of 170 wᵗʰ some few gentlemen voluntiers (who were all y° men in y° Collony y' were fitt for service) to march to Arctaba, where they und'stood 900. Spanyards, South sea men, were com to fall upon them by land. after 2 daies march he came up wth them, who Lay in a palisad fortification, whom he atackd, kild about 100 of them, took their Camp & gave them a total rout. The Governour of S! Maries, an old Spanish Soldier Lay in great fear. Leaving only eight men wth him. y° gentlemen Voluntiers pursued y° Spanyards till night, gave no quarter. 9 of y° Scots w' kild, most of them, gentlemen, y° Spanyards had laid at their Approach two Ambuscadoes, who took all their bagg & baggage, y° Governo'? plate & six pound of Gold dust. At theire return back to y° fortification they found 3000. Spanish Souldiers Landed wth 15 Saile of Ships of war, who lay two moneths of y° harbers mouth, to p'vent provitions Coming to their relief. There people being most of them Sick & their want of provisions fourced them to Surrender on Articles Viz. That they should depart wth all they had, & if any of their Ships Should com wthin 6 moneth they should have wood & water & depart in peace.

One Cap! Tho. Droumand, one of y° former Councel, in a Small Ship of 6 guns & 13 men met wth a Spanish man of war of 20 guns, ingaiged for four howers & faught his way thro y° fleet & got in to Callidonia, being Laden wth provissions, but y° fourt was surrendred before he Came. This is y° Substance of w' offers from

Your honours
most humble
Servant

After p'usual I beg   DUNCAN CAMPBELL.
   yo' honr' favour to Send
      it to y° postmaster m? Chandler

[Addressed]   To
The Honourable Coll. WINTHROP
Governour of Connetticut
at New London
Indorsed, — M' Campbell, May 28th 1700.   Free

* Galloones ammounts to £500,000 wth her majë has appropriated to the use of the Publick.

Lond? Jan'y 30, The K. of Spain refuises his Merch!' any of y° plate from Vigo, pretending first to make inquirey into the English & Dutches part.

Lond? Feb'7 2^d The Jnsurrection of y° Cevennes proving every Day more Considerable, the french K. sent a Marshall with 20.000 ag! The MaleContents, who grow daylie more numerous. They writt from Room of a great Earthquake Oblidged the Jnhabitants to leave their houses. That the Towns of Norica, Caretto, Coscia, Rietti, Spoleto, proligno and others are quite overturned, and a great number of people perished

Lond? Feb'7 4. An Embargo laid on throughout the Kingdome till the fleett is man'd.

Lond? Feb 7.5, The K. of france Proffered the Male Contents a par-

---

* This fragment is the continuation of a letter published in the Proceedings for March, 1867, p. 491, which concludes abruptly thus: — " Lond? Jan'7 23: Wee hear the Queen's Part of y° Galloons " . . . These words connect here. — EDS.

don, if would lay down their armes; if would not, order to Kill and
Destroy all.

It's said that the hono^ble Jn.° How Esqr and S.^r Jn.° Levingston Gowr
are to be Created peers, and that the Marqueis of Normanby, the E: of
Rochester, and the Ld Godolphin L^d treasurer to be made Dukes.

Letters say that the Grand Signeour has been Offered by the french
K. 50 Millions of Livers to breake wth the Emperour. He putts himselfe
into Warrlike preperations, to Obstruct the Muscovites entering his
territory's and to Reduce the Arabs who are in Rebellion.

The Bishop of Lincolns Lady flung herselfe out of a window this
afternoon and Dashed out her Braines.

Letters from Room say the Consternation is great because the Con-
tinuence of ye Earthquake, which has done the Ecclesiastick's a great
deal of Damage, and y^t 1500 persons were ruined in it.

The King of Poland and Cardinall primatt are Jsueing out Circular
Letters one ag^t the other Diet's, the Primat sydes wth the K. of Swee-
den.

Lond: Feby 11. Letters from Gueinzey say that Capt Comby from
N. yorke putt in there by Stress of Weather.

The K. of Prusia sent money to London to build a Calvinest Church
for his subjects.

Lond.° Feby 16. Letters from Parris say that the Spannards will
not suffer the Cardinall De Estrees to be neir the K. Where upon
ye french K. wrote that Court he is much surprized at their Behav-
iour, after his Great Exspence in Defending their Monarchy.

Admir^ll Graydon is appointed to succeed Admir^ll Benbow for the
West-Jndies with all Speed. Sr Stafford fairborne is for ever made
incapable of any Sea Command, for Declining to goe to the West
Indies.

Lond.° Feby 18; The Brasill fleett to Portugall is said to be Worth
2 Millions.

S.^r Jn.° Munden is said to be Resorted to his former Command.

Dampier, wth 2 Ships of 26 guns, is Sailed for the South Seas, wth the
Queen's Commission.

The Portugueise do daylie Exspect warr to be proclaimed against
france and Spain.

Boston, Capt Delbridge Will Sail for Lond.° within a fourthnight,
and Capt Dowse within a Month. Cap^ts Gillam, Coram and Robertson
Jn 2 months.

Capt Jn.° Bennett in a Ship 100 Tuns 4 guns, men Answerable,
sails for Barbados in 6 Weeks.

The Prize Ship of 150 Tuns, wth her Loading, at Rhoad Jsland, will
be Exposed to Sail on Tuesday the 11 Jnstant.

[Addressed]   To The Honble
                       JOHN WINTHROP Esqr.
                          Governour of Conecticut
                              N. London
                         Frank

Indorsed, — Publick occurrances
           May 3^d 1703

BOSTON, June 14ᵗʰ 1703.

On the 8ᵗʰ Instant the Assembly was adjourned unto the Last Wednesday of this month.

On the 9ᵗʰ His Excell. being accompanyed with Severall Gentlemen, went to his Goverm! of New hampshire.

On the 10ᵗʰ a Sloop from the Bay of Campeachy, brings no news.

On the 11 Esqʳ Bromfield mett wᵗʰ a Sore Mischance ; coming out of his Warehouse door, a Sloop Lying before his Warehouse door, the m! of the Sloop hoising up his boom, the Sail, being Loos to Dry it, gave such a Swing that it struck him upon his Shouldier, Brock his Collar bone, put his Shouldier out of joynt; was for sometime speechless wᵗʰ the Stroak, but it's hoped He'l Recover and do well.

On the 12ᵗʰ Arrived a Sloop from the Bay of Vandoras, one Lamson m! who sayes that Cap! Wheeler, that went hence for Jamaica, is Dead, his men all prest on board men of warr, and his Ship Hal'd up.

Cap! Blew from Rᵈ Island is arrived here this Day.

The Gosport and Gally is this Day sailed for Piscataqua.

Philad. May 28. arrived a Sloop in 22 Dayes from Antegua, in whom Came Cap! Roach, an Inhabitant of that Island, wᵗʰ his family to Settle here, brings the bad news of our forces leaving Guardilup untaken, wᵗʰ the Loss of about 1000 by Enemy and Sickness. The Day he sailed the Gener!! Arrived, who has lost his Eye Sight wᵗʰ some Disstemper, the rest of the fleett and forces were Exspected from Guardiloop, the Gene!! Layes the Miscarridge so to heart that it's thought he'l hardly Recover upon it. It's said that the men of warr that were at Guardiloop were all ordered home, and were to Sail the 29ᵗʰ may.

Some Prisoners that made theire Escape from Martinico to Antegua sayes that the french were fitting out abundance of privateers from that place, many of them Stout Vessells.

It's reported in the West Judies that mons! Ponti was daylie Exspected there wᵗʰ a Squadron of men of warr of 22 Sail, besydes other Vessells.

The 31 arrived here a Sloop from Jamaica, 28 Dayes passage, Admir!! Whetstone, wᵗʰ his Squadron, was at Jamaica, he's done nothing, only burnt a Ship the french took from us, and two privateer Sloops at Pettiquavis.

A fleett of merchtmen between 40 & 50 Sail und! Convoy of 2 or 3 men of warr was to sail in may from Jamaica to England.

N. Yorke June 7 : Last Week arrived here a Sloop from Coraso, 21 Dayes passage, sayes the Dutch have an open Trade wᵗʰ New Spain, and that the Governour of Coraso has stopt Cap! Wrightington & his Comp! who sailed from R. Island, on what pretence knows not.

Cap! Bond & Cap! Sinclair sails in a fourth Night or 3 Weeks for London.

Boston Cap! Travise sails to Day or Too morrow for London.

[Addressed]   To The Honᵇˡᵉ
                          JOHN WINTHROP Esqʳ.
                             Govʳ. of Connecticut
                                 N. London
                               Franke

To N London

From Piscataqua the 1ˢᵗ Jnstant acquainted that a party of our forces, under the Command of Livᵗ Coll March and Majᵗ Cutler, about 365, marched on Sabbath Last to Pigwakett, and are in hopes to hear of them in Two or Three Dayes.

That mʳ Henry Newman in a Sloop took up 3 French men in a burch Cannoo at Casko-bay, who are brought hither; upon Examination they Say that on the 8ᵗʰ May Last they came from Quebeck, where they were Souldiers, and run away from thence, because of bad usage, and Jntended to Boston for Protection, they say that they sold their Armes at Port Royall. However it's judged they had no good Design, and are now in prison.

They say that the Govᵗ of Canada is Dead, and that ther is 28 Compˢ at Quebeck, consisting of 30 men Each.

From Hartford acquainted that a post came Latly from Albany, who acqua[inted] that a Mohawk was come in from [the] Lake and sayes that the Govᵗ of Canada wᵗʰ 700 men was on this side the Lake, Designing to march and make a Descent on the Frontiers of N. England, but that an Express came to him as was going to march, acquainting him of a fleett of ships seen, wᶜʰ they Knew not whether friends or foes, upon wᶜʰ he and his army posted back again.

And from Springfield it's said the reason of their going back was, the mischeif wᶜʰ our Indians had Done at the Eastward had awakened our people to Secure our Frontiers.

Boston, no Ships arrived this Week & wee are in great fears of our mast fleett, the only hopes is that they came not out wᵗʰ the Grand fleett, as it's said they did.

Wee had an Eminent Delivery, on Satturday night, about 12 a Clocke at Night, a fire had Like to have brock out in a house neir to Capᵗ Williams.

To The Honᵇˡᵉ
JOHN WINTHROP Esqᵗ
Goᵗ of Connecticut at
N. London
Franck

Indorsed, — Mʳ Jonn Campbell's Newes
Oct. 4ᵗʰ 1703.

Mr. DEANE presented, in the name of Mr. J. Elliot Cabot, a plan of Fortifications on Bunker Hill and Charlestown Neck, which Mr. Cabot had found among the papers of the late Colonel Thomas H. Perkins. Mr. Deane said he supposed the plan referred to contemplated defences during the war of 1812, when fears were entertained of an attack by the enemy on Boston and the Navy Yard.

Mr. FROTHINGHAM concurred in this opinion.

The President called attention, before the adjournment, to a Correspondence between Governor James Bowdoin, of Massachusetts, and Captain Stanhope, of the Royal Navy, in 1785, which had recently been printed in the October number of the Historical and Genealogical Register. It had been taken from Schomberg's " Naval Chronology," published in London in 1802. It was not surprising that, after the lapse of eighty-seven years, nothing was remembered of this controversy. As a matter of fact, however, it was the subject of action, at the time, both in the Legislature of Massachusetts and in the Congress of the United States Confederation ; and the papers would be found in the printed journals of both those bodies. Some of the originals were in his own possession, with the family papers of Governor Bowdoin. Schomberg's account of the affair was very incomplete, and some of the letters were incorrectly printed. But he had not thought it important to revive the remembrance of the difficulty by reproducing papers which were already among the Legislative Documents of the country.

Mr. DEANE communicated a transcript of Captain John Smith's " New England's Trials," first edition, for publication in the Society's " Proceedings," and made the following observations respecting it : —

On my first visit to the Bodleian Library at Oxford, in 1866, the first book I asked to look at was Hariot's Virginia, 1588; and the second was the first edition of Captain John Smith's " New England's Trials," 1620, both of which I had understood to be in that library. These books are of exceeding rarity; and though the British Museum also has a copy of each, I am not aware that either can be found in this country. I had for some years possessed a copy of the second edition of the " Trials," 1622, which is the one usually cited. Considerable additions were made to the second edition. The first contains only eight leaves of text, while the second contains fourteen. Neither edition is paged. By the phrase, " New England's *Trials*," the author does not mean New England's afflictions or sufferings, but the *attempts* or *experiments* made in the prosecution of voyages thither for settlement or for fishing. The book was published four years after his " Description of New England," in which he gives an account of his only visit here two years before.

There is nothing in either edition to indicate that a map was published with it ; yet it seems most probable that Smith's map of New England, first issued in the " Description of New England," 1616, was reissued in both. The map is found in some of his later publications, and was also inserted as late as 1635

in Sparks's " Historia Mundi." The result of a collation of
many copies of the map, by Mr. Lenox and myself, has shown
that it was issued in at least nine different conditions, all from
the same copperplate, but additions and alterations were made
in the plate from time to time at subsequent issues of the map.
The map was first published in its simplest form in the " Description of New England," 1616. One of these may be seen
in a copy of this tract in the Prince Library. The second
issue of the map, it is conjectured, was published in the " New
England's Trials " of 1620. On this the date " 1614," the year
of Smith's visit to New England, was introduced under the
scale of leagues, as are " P. Travers " and " Gerrard Isles "
near Pembrock's Bay. These, so far as observed, are the only
additions to the map in its second stage. A lithographic
fac-simile of the map in this stage (except that a number of
ships in the body of it are wanting) is prefixed to the reprint
of Smith's " Advertisements," in 3 Mass. Hist. Coll., iii. 1.

The transcript of " New England's Trials " which I now
communicate to the Society has been made for me from a
copy of the original tract in the Bodleian Library.

It is quite unnecessary to dwell here on the well-known
career of Captain Smith. After living about two years and a
half in Virginia, he left that settlement in 1609, " about
Michaelmas,"—the last of September, for England, never to
return. We hear little further of him till, in 1614, he embarked for New England, then called North Virginia, " with two
ships, sent out," as he says, " at the charge of Captain Marma-
duke Roydon, Captain George Langam, M. John Buley, and W.
Skelton," merchants of London. " I went from the Downs the
third of March, and arrived in New England the last of April,
where I was to have stayed but with ten men to keep possession
of those large territories." (*New England's Trials, second ed.*)
He failed in making a settlement, and returned on the 18th
of July, arriving at Plymouth the latter end of August. He
brought back in the ship in which he sailed a large quantity
of fish, furs, and oil, and a map of the country which he had
drawn while there.

In March of the following year, 1615, Smith set sail from
Plymouth with two vessels, fitted out by Sir Ferdinando Gorges,
and others, for New England, where, " when the fishing was
done, only with fifteen I was to stay in the country ; but ill
weather breaking all my masts, I was forced to return to Plymouth." The other ship proceeded on her voyage. He then
re-embarked on the 24th of June in a vessel of sixty tons,
but was overtaken near Flores by some French men-of-war

and himself carried to France, returning to England before the close of the year. (*Ibid.* ; *Description of New England.*)

Smith never again embarked for New England. He says that great promises were held out to him by the Plymouth Company, or its members, but that they were never fulfilled. Two years later, under date of 1617, he says : —

"I being at Plymouth provided with 3 good ships, yet but fifteen men to stay with me in the country, was wind-bound three months, as was many a hundred sail more ; so that the season being past, the ships went for Newfound-land, whereby my design was frustrate, which was to me and my friends no small loss, in regard whereof here the Western Commissioners in the behalf of themselves and the rest of the Company, contracted with me by articles indented under our hands, to be Admiral of that Country during my life, and in the renewing of their Letters patents so to be nominated ; half the fruits of our endeavours theirs, the rest our own ; being thus ingaged, now the business doth prosper, some of them would willingly forget me ; but I am not the first they have deceived." (*New England's Trials, second ed.*)

In the last book which he wrote, published in 1631, the year of his death, in recurring to the year 1617, he says, "They promised me the next year twenty sail, well furnished, made me *Admiral* of the Country for my life, under their hands, and the Colony's Seal for *New England;* and in renewing their Letters Patents to be a Patentee for my pains, yet nothing but a volutary fishing was effected for all this air." (*Advertisements for the Unexperienced Planters, &c.*)

From Smith's own account in the above extracts from his books, it would appear that he was made Admiral of New England in 1617 ; but on the title-page of his "Description of New England," published the year before, "At London, *printed the* 18th *of June,* in the yeere of our Lord, 1616," he styles himself "Admirall of that Country;" and this title, following his name, was also inscribed on the map which accompanied this tract. He nowhere in the text speaks of having had this title conferred upon him ; but he says that, after his return from New England, and he had imparted his purposes relative to that country to Sir Ferdinando Gorges, and some others, at Plymouth, "I was so incouraged and assured to have the managing their authority in those parts, during my life, that I ingaged to undertake it for them" (p. 48).

Although Smith seems to have failed in maintaining for himself the confidence either of the Plymouth or the London Company, and was never again employed in the service of either, he continued his interest in the colonization of both colonies,

— at least he constantly sought employment, and wrote books and distributed them most liberally in furtherance of his objects.* In his "Generall Historie," published in 1624, after citing largely from his "New England's Trials," he says: "Now all these proofs and this relation I now called New *England's* trial. I caused two or three thousand of them to be printed; one thousand, with a great many maps both of *Virginia* and *New-England*, I presented to thirty of the chief Companies in *London*, at their Halls, desiring either generally or particularly (them that would) to imbrace it, and by the use of a stock of five thousand pound, to ease them of the superfluity of the most of their companies that had but strength and health to labour; near a year I spent to understand their resolutions, which was to me a greater toil and torment than to have been in *New England* about my business, but with bread and water, and what I could get there by my labour; but, in conclusion, seeing nothing would be effected, I was contented as well with this loss of time and charges as all the rest " (p. 230).

A brief summary of the condition of affairs as to the colonization of New England, from the time of the breaking up of the Popham Colony in 1608, to the settlement at Plymouth in 1620, will conclude this prefatory note. It is taken from Smith's " True Travels," published in 1630 : —

"When I went first to the North part of *Virginia*, where the Westerly Colony had been planted, it had dissolved it self within a year, and there was not one *Christian* in all the land.† I was set forth at the sole charge of four merchants of *London*; the Country being then reputed by your westerlings a most rocky, barren, desolate desart; but the good return I brought from thence, with the maps and relations I made of the Country, which I made so manifest, some of them did believe me, and they were well embraced, both by the Londoners, and Westerlings, for whom I had promised to undertake it, thinking to have joyned them all together, but that might well have been a work for *Hercules*. Betwixt them long there was much contention; the Lon-

---

* Sometime in the year 1618, Smith addressed a letter to Lord Bacon (now preserved in the Public Record Office in London), in which he solicits his lordship's patronage, "humbly desiring your Honor would be pleased to grace me with the title of your lordship's servant." He enlarges upon his own former services and sacrifices in the cause of colonization, and promises to effect great things towards this object if means and opportunity were provided him. He hopes his "poverty" may be no hindrance to the success of his application. He gives in the letter some statistics, showing the success which had attended the fishing-vessels sent to the coast of New England the previous four years, and much in the same language which he employs on the fourth and fifth pages of his "New England's Trials," published two years afterwards. (*Memorial Volume of the Popham Celebration*, App. pp. 104–107, Portland, 1863.)

† Smith means that there was no settlement or colony of Christians there. He himself speaks of other fishing-vessels being on the coast at the time he was there.

doners indeed went bravely forward; but in three or four years, I and my friends consumed many hundred pounds amongst the *Plymothians*, who only fed me but with delays, promises, and excuses, but no performance of any thing to any purpose. In the interim, many particular ships went thither, and finding my relations true, and that I had not taken that I brought home from the French men, as had been reported; yet further for my pains to discredit me, and my calling it *New-England*, they obscured it, and shadowed it, with the title of *Canada*, till at my humble suit, it pleased our most Royal King *Charles*, whom God long keep, bless, and preserve, then Prince of *Wales*, to confirm it with my map and book, by the title of *New England*; the gain thence returning did make the fame thereof so increase that thirty, forty, or fifty sail, went yearly only to trade and fish; but nothing would be done for a plantation, till about some hundred of your Brownists of *England, Amsterdam*, and *Leyden*, went to *New-Plimouth*, whose humorous ignorances, caused them for more than a year, to endure a wonderful deal of misery, with an infinite patience; saying my books and maps were much better cheap to teach them, than my self; many other have used the like good husbandry that have payed soundly in trying their selfwilled conclusions; but those in time doing well, diverse others have in small handfulls undertaken to go there, to be several Lords and Kings of themselves, but most vanished to nothing," &c. (pp. 46, 47).

A little further on he says: "Now this year 1629, a great company of people of good rank, zeal, means, and quality, have made a great stock; and with six good ships, in the months of April and May, they set sail from [the] *Thames*, for the Bay of the *Massachusetts*," &c. They were bound for Salem, to supply Endicott, who had arrived there the year before; and they were followed the next year by the fleet under Winthrop.

[Smith's tract will be found at the end of the volume, following page 447, reprinted page for page according to the original. The vignettes and the ornamented initial letters are not *fac-similes*.]

.

www.ingramcontent.com/pod-product-compliance
Lightning Source LLC
Chambersburg PA
CBHW031750090426
42739CB00008B/952